Full-Time Woman
Part-Time Career

Launching a Flexible Business That Fits Your Life,
Feeds Your Family and Fuels Your Brain

By Karen Steede Terry

CMS
Press

2006

Disclaimer

This book is published as a general reference and is intended to complement, supplement, and augment other available texts. It contains information from many sources, including personal experiences on the part of the author and interview subjects; it is understood that the strategies presented herein may not be suitable for everyone or for every circumstance. Furthermore, this book is sold with the understanding that neither the author nor publisher are engaged in rendering any legal, psychological, or accounting advice. Although every effort has been made to ensure the completeness and accuracy of this manuscript, the publisher and author assume no responsibility or liability for any errors, inaccuracies, omissions, inconsistencies, or loss or damage caused by information or advice contained in this book.

Publisher's Cataloging-in-Publication
(Provided by Quality Books, Inc.)

Steede-Terry, Karen.
 Full-time woman, part-time career: launching a
 flexible business that fits your life, feeds your family
 and fuels your brain / by Karen Steede Terry.
 p. cm.
 Includes bibliographical references and index.
 ISBN 0-9760589-0-1

 1. Home-based business. 2. Women-owned business
enterprises. 3. New business enterprises. I. Title.

HD62.38.S74 2005   658.1'1412'082
                                     QBI04-200368

Full-Time Woman, Part-Time Career
ISBN-13: 978-0-9760589-0-8
ISBN-10: 0-9760589-0-1
Library of Congress Control Number: 2005906132

Published by

CMS Press
(Capitol Metropolitan Signature Press)
P.O. Box 500273
Austin, TX 78750

Cover Photo of the Author by Evin Thayer Studios, Houston, Texas

DEDICATION

For my daughter –
may your world be rich with opportunity, possibility, and happiness.

Table of Contents

Acknowledgements

First and foremost, I would like to express my appreciation to all of the case studies. I especially appreciate their willingness to participate in this project. Without their cooperation, knowledge, insights, and advice this book would not be what it is. You will find those women acknowledged by name at the end of their respective chapters.

I spoke to several people who were not featured as case studies; nevertheless their experiences contributed immensely to the overall book. Even though they may or may not be mentioned specifically by name, thanks are due all of them. You will find their stories sprinkled throughout the introduction and subsequent chapters.

I also extend my gratitude to colleagues, clients, and friends. If you had never asked me for advice, the idea for this book would've never been born!

There are a few additional people I would like to thank: *Full-Time Woman, Part-Time Career* would not exist without the hard work of Michele Mason, who did the page layout and book design. Thank you Michele, for all of your patience during the "tweaking" process. Robin McDonald designed the cover. Mim Eisenberg proofed and edited the text. Peter Bowerman, for his coaching, guidance, and brutal honesty. Sam Horn, for taking the time to help me make this a better book. Jayne, for helping me with Chapter 8. Thanks are also due to Evin Thayer and his helpful staff (Dennis, Patrick, and Jennifer) for the cover photo.

I would also like to thank my family for giving me the time to complete this project; especially my husband David – you are a wonderful husband and father.

Introduction

Over the past few years, I have had many women approach me for advice about starting their own business. These women wanted to "pick my brain" and copy my business model.

I found this amusing, because I never even knew that I had a business model! All were seeking a part-time professional career that would allow them to work from home while raising a family.

For a variety of reasons, increasing numbers of women are looking for more flexibility not only in a career, but in their daily lives as well. Sound familiar?

All of these women – from recently married professional women thinking about starting a family, to women with three kids who quit a corporate career – are looking for viable, part-time career options they can pursue while they have children and raise a family. Chances are, since you picked up this book, you are one of them. Does this describe you:

- Are you working more than 40 hours a week?
- Do you have technical, programming, or other computer skills?
- Are you a woman working in a male-dominated industry?
- Would you like to earn income commensurate with your talent and experience?
- Are you tired of commuting?
- Would you like to work from home?
- Do you "freeze up" at the thought of trying to give a presentation or make sales?

- Have you dreamed of becoming your own boss?
- Are you worried about giving up your benefits, including health insurance?
- Are you looking for a way out of the corporate work world?
- Are you a former career woman turned stay-at-home mom, whose children are now in school and you're looking for a way to ease back into the working world?
- Are you wondering if you will have to change careers entirely or is there something else out there that you can do using your existing skills?
- Would you like to earn good money and have more time to spend with your family?

If you can answer "yes" to any of the above questions, then this book is for you! *Full-Time Woman, Part-Time Career* is written specifically for married professional women who want to transition to part-time work and/or a more flexible lifestyle. Sound good?

You may be wondering what it is that I do that is so attractive to women who want more flexibility in their life?

I am self-employed, and I teach computer software classes. Teaching! What about that old saying, "Those who can, do, and those who can't, teach"? Not so! On the contrary, you have to know a subject extremely well in order to teach it. The same is true for consulting, public speaking, coaching, and sales. Technically, it's called being a "Subject Matter Expert," or SME.

MY STORY

In 1996, I quit my job, married, and moved from Houston, Texas, to Austin, the state capital. Nestled in the Texas Hill Country, and appropriately nicknamed "Silicon Hills," at the time Austin was undergoing a tremendous high-tech economic boom. Even so, the smaller metropolitan area offered few employment opportunities in my field.

At first, I worked for a small consulting company on a contract basis. After a few months, the company went through a difficult financial period and consequently laid off a good portion of its staff, including all contractors. Not having a full-time job, I decided to explore what I could do out on my own "for a little while." Today I have built my own business writing, teaching, and consulting in two specialized, but interrelated, fields known as Geographic Information Systems (GIS) and Global Positioning Systems (GPS).

When I started out, I certainly did not foresee creating a business model that other women would want to copy. However, now that I have a daughter of my own, I have come to appreciate the flexibility that my line of work offers. I truly have the best of both worlds – ample income and time with my daughter. I want to share my knowledge, experience, and insights with you so that you can do it too!

If all of this sounds easy, I want to set the record straight. Many of the women who originally approached me wanting to "do what I do" only see the part where I teach a few times a month. What they don't see is everything that goes on behind the scenes.

I have one colleague who started out on her own, but she didn't do enough to market herself and ultimately didn't make it. I don't want this to happen to you. *Full-Time Woman, Part-Time Career* tells you exactly what you need to know and do to go out on your own, including how to sell yourself and your services.

There are many books on balancing a career with motherhood (is there really such a thing?) or starting a home-based business. However, while most work-from-home opportunities involve stuffing envelopes, assembling crafts, or selling cosmetics or kitchen accessories from well-known companies, these are not necessarily appealing options for all women.

Full-Time Woman, Part-Time Career takes a different approach by bridging the gap for women who are looking for flexible, professional, and technical career options. And, unlike those other businesses, you don't have to come up with a significant amount of money up-front to buy products. I believe that, using the strategies outlined in this book, women can build a part-time business in as little as two years, in order to have a more flexible and satisfying life. But first, let's define part time.

"Part-time" means different things to different people. In traditional income models, people work 40 hours or more per week, and earn a standard annual salary, paid weekly or monthly. Working part time doesn't necessarily mean working only 20 hours or less a week.

Some of the women profiled in the book work only a few hours per day, or one or two days each week. Cynthia Long, a project manager featured in Chapter 3, defines part-time work as working on a project for several months in a row, and then having several months off. What it boils down to is building up your business to realize the payoff of having flexibility in your life.

Once a woman has her first child, she faces a difficult decision – whether or not to stay home with her child, or go back to work. There is no perfect solution. Becoming a full-time stay-at-home mom is not the answer for everyone. Some can easily transition from the professional workplace to full-time motherhood with no problems. For others, it is not that easy. Some need to keep working in order to retain their sense of identity and self-worth and/or to keep their mind active.

A married friend of mine, who chose to stay home full time with her two boys after working for many years in the computer field, summarizes the mixed feelings that many women wrestle with:

> Not all women can give up their work. I find that both sides [women who continue to work after having children, and those who don't] have things they are unhappy with.
>
> After the birth of my first child, I was planning on going back to work. I had three months of maternity leave and when I was down to the last week left, I was not ready to go back. I had received a huge pay raise at my job, and it was very attractive to go back.
>
> You give up a lot staying home, though. Yes, your children come first, but you do give up a part of yourself. I could never get a job now and make what I was making. I would have to start back at entry level. I try not to think about it and just go for the 'now.' I also hate being dependent upon someone else's money. I like earning my own money. Some days, I feel like all I do is laundry, cook and clean. It's easy not to feel appreciated. But I tell myself that it is all worth it in the end! My kids don't know how lucky they are to have their mom around all the time.

Professional women in particular are finding it increasingly difficult to choose between a career and the role of a traditional stay-at-home mom.

Not solely wives and mothers anymore, women today are multi-faceted – they have unprecedented access to higher education, birth control, and professional opportunities. As a result, many are delaying having families until later in life.

The U.S. Census Bureau reports that 19% of women aged 40-44 are childless, a number twice as high as twenty years ago. More women are postponing having a child until their mid thirties or early forties, thus waiting to start a family at an age when fertility rates plummet. This is likely a direct result of the increasing dilemma that women face: choosing to invest in a career versus raising a family.

Those who have spent time and money achieving a college education don't want to risk losing their skills or knowledge if they quit working in favor of staying home full time. Others marry later in life and thus have invested many years in a career before having children. And for others, due to the high cost of living in our society, staying home full time and living on one income is simply not financially feasible.

Or are you one of the thousands who has been laid off or whose job has been outsourced to a foreign country? According to the McKinney Global Institute, $57 billion worth of Information Technology (IT) and professional service jobs (e.g., accounting work) will be exported to India or other countries by 2008 (*BusinessWeek*, December 8, 2003).

Why not create your own job security by going out on your own? Many people who are laid off later claim that the experience was "the best thing that could've happened" to them. Or maybe you're just looking for a way out of the corporate rat race. In any case, there is a growing trend among women to shun the traditional "9 to 5" work model and do something more flexible on their own.

Full-Time Woman, Part-Time Career offers women options, viable professional and technical careers they can start out of their house, and offers a compromise for those who don't want to give up their career completely in order to stay home. The book explores available professional career options for women who want to go into business for themselves, and features tips and advice for getting started and building a business, regardless of what field you are in.

Interspersed throughout the book are interviews with six successful women – all "full-time women" with children and very busy lives who were able to make this work – from a wide range of fields who escaped the corporate work world and now have flexible schedules because they started their own business. All offer their invaluable wisdom, insights, and advice to other women who want to create a more flexible lifestyle while raising a family. Their stories are included to inspire others and to demonstrate that having a "part-time career" is truly an attainable goal.

CHAPTER 1

Getting Started:
Do you have what it takes?

Make no mistake about it, starting your own business can be a terrifying experience. When I first started out, I had been let go from a consulting firm that I had been working for on a contract basis. It was a period of high anxiety for me. (I recently read an article that said you are on the verge of great change when you experience anxiety.)

Up until that time, the firm had been my only client, and I didn't have anything else lined up. Two months prior, my husband and I had just closed on a new home, which took both our incomes to maintain. I literally panicked. "I HAVE to pay the mortgage!" ran through my head like a screaming freight train.

Fortunately, I still had my training certifications, so that evening I got right on the phone and began calling people and companies I used to work with (anybody I knew) asking if they needed training. First, I called a former colleague who now worked in sales for another company. Here is what I said:

> "Hi Mike. This is Karen. How are things going with your new job?
>
> The reason I am calling is to let you know that I have started my own business offering certified GPS training. Do you have any clients who need my services?"

As it turns out, he did, but I didn't stop there. I kept on calling and was on the phone until 10:00 P.M. that first night. The effort paid off, and the next thing I knew, I suddenly had two jobs lined up over the coming weeks. That is how I got started.

Notice in the preceding exchange, I purposely asked my colleague about his new job, hoping that things were going well. It paid off, because he happened to be very busy and needed someone (me!) who could train his customers on the products he was selling. In my case, my former colleague already knew me, knew that I was credible, and knew he could count on me to deliver the goods, so to speak.

The following telephone sales script can be modified to fit any situation, even for cold calls (people who do not know you):

> "Hello, My name is _____. I am calling to let you know that I am a _____ (certified instructor, trainer, computer consultant, etc.) and offer the following (classes, services, products). My services can benefit _____ (you, your company, your clients) by _____ (saving time, saving money, lowering costs, increasing productivity, you name it). Who can I talk to within your organization that can use my services? Do you have any clients you can refer me to?"

Going out on your own requires one key factor: motivation. For me, my motivation was suddenly having no income, but also knowing that I was still obligated to pay next month's mortgage payment. Many people find it easy to sit back in a comfy cozy job and daydream about going out on their own or eventually starting their own business, but to actually *do it* is another matter. You must be motivated.

How do you overcome that hurdle if you aren't? By wanting to make a lifestyle change. For many women, having enough time to stay home with a new baby is a powerful motivator.

In addition to motivation, going out on your own takes an enormous commitment and a lot of hard work, as well as an entrepreneurial spirit, and the right combination of perseverance, persistence and patience; personal sacrifice, maturity, self-confidence, innovation, and, (if you are going to try computer consulting), technical competency. WOW – that sure is a long list! Let's tackle each quality one at a time.

TOP TEN QUALITIES REQUIRED TO GO OUT ON YOUR OWN OR START A BUSINESS

1. Motivation.
2. Commitment.
3. Hard Work.
4. Perseverance, Persistence and Patience.
5. Personal Sacrifice.
6. Maturity/Self-Discipline.
7. Self-Confidence.
8. Innovation/Niche Market.
9. Technical Competency/Proficiency.
10. Be Business-Minded.

COMMITMENT

If you're really going to go out on your own, then you must make a commitment and be dedicated to your business. Your business must be a top priority in your life, especially when starting out.

A woman I know is trying to build up her business (having copied my business model), but she doesn't really take it seriously. One Friday morning I had some referral business I was going to send her way, so I called her with a hot lead. When she did not answer, I left a voice mail message, asking her to call me. Instead of returning my call, she sent me an e-mail stating that is was too difficult to return my call because she was preparing to have company over the weekend.

Guess what? I called someone else and gave them the business. In the time it took for her to write the e-mail, she could've called me back and gained some new business. It was obvious to me that since she didn't consider her business a higher priority than her weekend guests, then she probably would not give my client good service. Ultimately, I couldn't risk her being unresponsive and potentially damaging my own reputation.

Lesson learned? Be responsive and professional: make a commitment to return all phone calls (and e-mails) promptly. Opportunity doesn't always knock! If you are not responsive, then your customers will go elsewhere and you will lose business and income.

It goes without saying that starting a business is a full-time job. When I first started out, I was working much more than 40 hours a week to build up the business. You will be, too. Keep in mind that you are everything, from accountant, receptionist, marketing and salesperson, all in addition to being the primary consultant for hire.

It's an easy misconception to think you are going to start out working two or three days a week consulting or teaching classes. There's a lot more to it than that. It requires commitment and dedication and being in the office at least five days a week. Someone once asked me, "What do you do when you are not teaching?" My answer was, "Run a business."

When you are self-employed, there is always something you can be doing. If you don't understand this basic premise, then you should not go out on your own. There is always something you can do to market yourself and build your business (see Chapter 4: Selling Yourself for more tips). It's a lot of hard work, and you will not be working part time at first.

That's an important concept, so let me restate it: you will not be working part time initially. If you plan to become pregnant, it would be wise to start your business at least two years prior to your first pregnancy. This helps you get into the swing of things and learn how to run your business before the baby comes along (when your life will be turned upside down!). Most women I have talked to say that it can take anywhere from six months to two years (sometimes longer) to really build your business, and it's simply not realistic to plan on working when you have a newborn.

I believe that once you become established and build up your business to the point where you don't have to prospect; you can just take the calls that come in, and work part time. But you must build up the business first, to get to the point where you have a lot of referrals (Note: In a sense, you will always be building your business).

After my daughter was born, I effectively cut back my business to part time by limiting my travel and accepting only in-town assignments. Today, I truly have the best of both worlds, but only because I did the hard part (building my business during the start-up phase) before becoming pregnant.

PERSEVERANCE, PERSISTENCE, AND PATIENCE

Perseverance, persistence, and patience. Every good salesperson knows these three keys to successful selling. It may take six months, or more, but keep at it, and your clients will begin to come in the proverbial door.

PERSONAL SACRIFICE

Starting your own business is not a "get rich quick" scheme. It doesn't work that way. It requires a tremendous amount of personal sacrifice, sometimes a lot more than you ever imagined. It can take two years to get started, and may take up to ten years before you begin to build any wealth.

Be ready to "do without." When I first started out, I did not have any income for three months. (Even though I had jobs right away, it can still take anywhere from 30 to 90 days to get paid.) I was living off less than a $1000 a month (2/3 of which went to our mortgage payment), pulled from savings. Fortunately, I drove a car that I had already paid off. I ended up driving it for more than six years before purchasing a new one.

A man I know declared he was going to start his own business. At the time, he needed an $8000 piece of equipment to get started. (For more on start-up costs, see Chapter 2.) He said he didn't have the money, but then he promptly went out and bought his wife a brand-new SUV.

Your priority must be your business. Granted, $8000 is quite a bit of money, however, you must be willing to sacrifice owning some material possessions now for a potentially bigger payoff later. Someone once told me, "Don't start your own business unless you are serious and willing to sell everything you own, your house, your car, everything!" Good advice, I thought.

MATURITY AND SELF-DISCIPLINE

Do you have the maturity and self-discipline to go out on your own? There won't be any boss looking over your shoulder. It will be up to you to sit down and get the work done.

One recommendation is to have a set work schedule and regular office hours. Even if you work at home, get up and get dressed for work every day. This takes self-discipline. Establish good work habits and a daily routine which doesn't include the temptation to watch TV or putter around in the garden when you're supposed to be working.

One other aspect of maturity involves developing the necessary communication skills to deal with clients (more on this in Chapter 14). If you burst into tears the minute someone criticizes you, or tend to avoid conflict, those ingrained behaviors are not going to work once you go into business for yourself. You must control your emotions and be business-minded and professional.

Not only must you provide excellent customer service, but you must also be able to listen to your customers, acknowledge them, and understand and interpret their needs. This is crucial in order to sell your services. One of the best books on that topic is the classic *How to Win Friends and Influence People*, by Dale Carnegie (Pocket Books, 1981). This is an excellent guide to understanding people and developing interpersonal skills.

SELF-CONFIDENCE

Self-confidence. It's easy to doubt yourself when you first start out and you don't have any business or clients yet. It's a very vulnerable time, the equivalent of being unemployed and looking for a job. The difference in this case is that you are a consultant for hire, one who has specialized skills and knowledge. Consultants are worthy of their rate and know it. Adopt this attitude and make a conscious decision to be successful.

How do you cope with the "terrors," that awful feeling in the pit of your stomach that comes from not having any work or income? This is by far the scariest part of self-employment, making that leap from steady paycheck to not having any regular income. It helps to know that experiencing some anxiety is normal. One way is to create or insure that there is demand for the product or service you are offering before starting out. The other way is to believe in yourself and what you are doing. In other words, have self-confidence.

Tina Brown, who started her own consulting business, and is profiled in Chapter 7, has this to say about the "terrors": "When I was younger, I felt that the jobs would go away and/or the money would go away. Now I don't think that anymore. Once you get going, your business gains momentum, and the jobs will keep coming in."

Starting out, if you are married, it is assumed that you will have a working spouse. That way, you will still have some income coming in the door once you quit your job. You can work from home, and transfer over to you husband's health insurance. It also helps to have some money saved up to get through the initial start-up phase.

INNOVATION

One thing that helps to quickly build momentum is having a unique niche or an innovative idea. If you have something that no one else offers, obviously your services or product will be in high demand. My niche is GIS and GPS; and when I started out, nobody else was training on the combined technologies.

Another way to look at this is to compare Home Depot to a smaller specialty hardware store. While Home Depot may carry almost everything you need, they are not as likely to have unique or hard-to-find items. These items may cost more at a specialty store, however, that is the niche market that sets the specialty store apart. This concept is referred to as product differentiation.

Cynthia Long, who specializes in project management, and is profiled in Chapter 3, talks about finding her niche. "I worked in a number of different kinds of roles when I was in full-time employment. I learned about myself. People who worked for me told me that I was a good manager. I enjoyed project management. It had a start and a finish (was a finite thing), and then someone else takes over the maintenance. I discovered that my strength is starting and implementing the project, but not maintaining it. I found I was glad to hand it off. That's why I focus on project management. I see a problem being addressed and fixed, and that is very satisfying to me."

TECHNICAL COMPETENCY CHECKLIST

Now let's tackle technical competency, as well as a few additional qualities. I can hear you asking, but don't I have to know how to set up a computer network or perform some other administrative computer task? Sure, it helps to be computer savvy or have technical expertise in your field (and I assume that you do), but there is more to it than that. Ask yourself these questions:

1. Are you ready, with your skills and positive attitude, to go out on your own and start a business?
2. Are you prepared possibly to go several months without any income?
3. Are you a problem solver?
4. Are you flexible and adaptable? Can you think quickly on your feet?
5. Are you somewhat of a maverick (non-conformist) who bucks authority, and/or someone who frequently finds a way around bureaucracy in order to attain results?

6. Do others use you as a technical resource and/or ask you for advice?
7. Are you competent with computers?
8. Are you a guru with a specialized piece of software?
9. Are you resourceful and/or do you often see more than one solution to a problem?
10. Are you well-known and well-regarded in your industry or field?
11. Do you exhibit grace under pressure when faced with a difficult situation, a complex technical problem, or a tough technical question you can't answer immediately?
12. Do you have someone to call when you don't know the answer to a technical question? In other words, do you have a backup person or a technical support hotline that you can fall back on?
13. Are you ready and do you enjoy taking on new challenges?

If you can answer yes to these questions and feel comfortable relying on yourself (there's that self-confidence again), then you are ready to go out on your own.

A few parting words about getting started. Be willing to take on work that wouldn't normally appeal to you. Later you can afford to be choosy, but at first you may be doing jobs that you don't want to do, just to have money coming in the door and to build up your reference list.

Establish and maintain a network of contacts, and don't burn any bridges. Always end business arrangements amicably and keep in touch periodically – you never know when they might need you again. Follow up on every lead that comes your way, and be grateful for any work that comes in as a result of that lead. Acknowledge and say "thank you" to your clients and to people who refer you. These small things can make a big difference in whether you succeed or fail.

CHAPTER 2

The Nuts and Bolts
of Starting a Business

Okay, so you've decided to make the big leap. Congratulations on your decision! Now what? It's time to tackle the logistics of getting started.

START-UP COSTS AND OTHER DECISIONS

In 1996, the year I started out on my own, I took $6000 out of my savings account (I had worked previously as a sales rep, and had saved all of my commissions) and placed the money into a dedicated business checking account. Half of that, I immediately used to purchase a laptop computer, a printer, a fax machine, business cards, and miscellaneous other office supplies. I remember paying around $1500 for a state-of-the-art laptop computer – at the time, the latest model with nearly a gigabyte hard drive! Printers were about $500, and once I was finished, I had exactly half of my start-up funds left to pay myself until I could drum up some business.

Fortunately the price of computers, printers, and other electronics are priced much lower today, and it is possible to start a business without a large up-front capital investment. There are ads on television for Dell computers and other brands starting at $999. Some are priced even lower, or higher, depending on memory and hard disk size.

If you are going to teach software classes you will need a laptop or notebook computer and a PowerPoint projector. One of your business expenses will be a copy of the software you are going to teach, and also any certifications you need to teach it (see Chapter 11 for more information).

You can purchase a combination printer/fax/scanner/copier, rather than three or four separate pieces of equipment. So, start-up costs today for all equipment and supplies (aside from the projector) can easily total only about $1500, which is what I paid back in 1996 for just the computer alone. (Hint: Chances are you will make back these initial costs pretty quickly).

Be sure to order some professional business cards. Apply for a business credit card so you can track your business expenses and keep them separate. You can also apply for an additional personal credit card and use it exclusively for business expenses.

SET UP AN OFFICE

Many people start out by setting up a home office. This is a cost-effective solution. For more on the pros and cons of working from home, see Chapter 16.

Once you have purchased a computer, fax machine, and/or printer, you will need a phone. Consider getting a mobile phone and using it as a dedicated office line. Most calling plans cost the same or less than a business line and include long distance calls.

Drawbacks to using a mobile phone are that calls are not always as clear as on a land line. Sometimes calls are dropped due to poor signal strength, which would be embarrassing if you're in the middle of a conversation with a client.

HEALTH INSURANCE

If you are married, immediately transfer over to your husband's health insurance after quitting your job. Some companies will not carry a spouse on their insurance if the spouse has coverage available at her own place of employment.

On the flip side, sometimes there is a time limit if you wait too long after you quit your job to get on your husband's insurance. In either case, there will likely be a waiting period before the insurance company will pay for pre-existing conditions. If you have to purchase your own health insurance for your company, it can easily cost hundreds or even thousands of dollars.

DEVELOP A BUSINESS PLAN

Starting out, you must have a business plan, which is an internal document that guides the entrepreneur or business owner along the path to success. Putting your ideas in writing is the first step to achieving your goals. There are many books available on how to write a detailed business plan, but in general, a business plan should include the following:

1. Title Page – identifies the name of the business.
2. Executive Summary – usually one page, identifying the purpose of the business, and its short-term and long-term goals.
3. Table of Contents – including page numbers.
4. Description of the Business – explains who you are, what the business will do, and who the intended customer is.
5. Products or Services Offered – explains what benefit the customer receives by buying from you.
6. Market/Competitive Analysis – provides an overview of the industry, customers, market, and competition. How is what you do different from other existing businesses? Do you have a niche?
7. Marketing Strategy – how will you sell your services?
8. Production Processes – how do you plan to deliver the good or services your business provides?
9. Management and Personnel – who are the key players and what are their roles? Include any subcontractors you plan to use.
10. Financial Data – include start-up costs and sources of funding.
11. Summary/Conclusions – summarizes major points in your plan and how you will achieve them.
12. Any Supporting Documents – resumes, incorporation papers, etc.

As you can see, by actually sitting down and putting some thought into the above topics, you can begin to formulate a solid plan. Research shows that companies with a solid business plan are less likely to fail during tough economic times. This was true for the dot-com companies that survived the bust in the early part of the 21st century. Planning is important. As the old saying goes, "If you fail to plan, you plan to fail."

SELLING SERVICES OR PRODUCTS

The process of writing a business plan makes you consider ideas or topics you may not have thought through before. One of these is whether or not to sell products or services, or both.

When I started out, I made a deliberate decision not to sell the software that I teach. I had several reasons for making my decision. One, there were already many dealers out there already selling the software. I did not want to compete with them; rather, I wanted to partner with them, and have them refer me to teach the software to the customer after they made the sale. At the time, this arrangement was unique; nobody else was offering training only. (I might add that nobody thought my idea could work, either).

Second, when I worked in sales, I saw firsthand what the dealers put up with, as far as backstabbing and competition with each other (and sometimes the manufacturer!), and I wanted no part of it. Third, I do not like paperwork, and any time I can take a shortcut to get out of it, I will. I did not want to deal with the paperwork, small profit margins, and up-front investment required to sell software.

Ann Kasunich, a marketing professional profiled in Chapter 10, offers her opinion on selling products vs. services: "It took me three months to figure out what I wanted to do (business-wise), and find my identity and figure out what services I wanted to offer. Ultimately, I decided not to resell software because I personally didn't think it would be very challenging, and the profit margins are so small."

Keep in mind that everybody is different. You may find that you love sales. One benefit of selling software is that it can provide you with a constant revenue stream.

If you do decide to sell software, apply for a sales tax and a reseller certificate through your state government's tax office. In most states, sales tax must be collected on all items sold, including software and course manuals. A state application must be filed that authorizes a business to collect sales tax from its customers. Check with your state comptroller's office for specific requirements, as different states levy tax on different items.

A reseller certificate grants you tax-exempt status for certain purchases. For instance, if you are selling software to a state agency or the federal government, those entities are tax exempt. If the software you sell comes from a third party company (in other words your company didn't invent the software, you bought it from another entity), then you will want to claim "reseller status" so that you do not have to pay up-front sales tax on the software you buy from them. In this case, your customer (the buyer) must furnish you with a tax-exempt certificate.

At the end of the calendar year, you will be required to file a state sales tax return, listing all of the purchases your customers made from you in the prior year. Again, check with your state comptroller's office for specific forms and other requirements.

TO INCORPORATE OR NOT TO INCORPORATE?

Before you start out, you will have to decide how you want your business to be *structured*. There are two basic business structures (and variations thereof): a sole proprietorship and a corporation. The most likely scenario for an independent consultant is a sole proprietor, which is simply you as an individual; this is also the simplest business structure.

As a sole proprietor, you and the company are one and the same. All profits pass through you personally and you declare them on your Form 1040 tax return using a Schedule C. To do business as a sole proprietor, take a trip down to your county courthouse or annex and register an assumed name certificate for your business. This is also known as a "DBA" (Doing Business As). The name you select will be the name that goes on your business cards.

If you decide to operate as a sole proprietor, there are a few things you need to know. If you hire any subcontractors to work for you, you will be responsible for issuing them an annual Form 1099, which reports the exact amount you paid the subcontractor. (Subcontractors are responsible for paying their own taxes.) At the same time, you will need to fill out a 1098 Form, reporting the same amount to the IRS. In turn, when you do a job for someone else, you will be required to fill out a W-9 Form, so that he/she can report to the IRS what they paid you.

Pay yourself a set amount each month, just as though you were on salary. In addition, you will be responsible for paying a percentage of your estimated gross income every quarter to the federal government. It is a good idea to set aside a certain percentage of each check you receive. According to Suze Orman, author of *The Nine Steps to Financial Freedom* (Crown Publishers, 1997), paying taxes quarterly is the preferred way to pay your taxes because you can set aside the money earmarked for taxes in an interest-bearing account and earn interest on it before that money is due to the IRS!

Speaking of taxes, every expense you incur to get (and keep) your business going as a sole proprietor is a tax write-off. This includes mileage, postage, taking a client to lunch, telephone bills, etc. Be sure to keep all of your receipts and accurate records of your expenses. Excel or another program such as Quicken or Quick Books can be used to keep track of your expenses electronically.

Use IRS Form SS-4 to apply for an Employer Identification Number (EIN), which keeps you from having to give out your social security number every time you do a job. In this age of identity theft, and easy access to personal and financial information, this is a safe precaution.

The second type of business structure is the corporation. A corporation is a separate tax-paying entity, filing its own tax return. (This is in addition to your personal income tax return.) There are different types of corporations: an "Inc." after your business name means "incorporated." An "LLC" is a Limited Liability Corporation, which protects the owner from personal liability, while allowing profits to pass through to the owner's personal income tax return. The drawback to an LLC is that it is not available in all states. A subchapter S corporation is the most popular corporate structure. It allows you the protection of a corporation, while allowing income to pass through to the owner's personal tax return.

There are arguments for and against incorporating. Corporations, by their very nature, are complex entities that require a lot of paperwork in order to preserve the identity of the corporation. If you decide to incorporate, hire a lawyer or a CPA to give you more information and to file the papers for you.

How do you know which structure is right for you? For most sole proprietors, the corporate structure is more than you need. The drawback to being a sole proprietor is that if for some reason, you are sued, your personal assets are at risk.

Corporate shareholders, by contrast, are exempt from any personal liability. For many, this is reason enough to set up a corporation. Beni Patel, profiled in Chapter 15, maintains that incorporating gives you greater credibility (see Chapter 4 for more tips on establishing credibility). Ultimately, it will be up to you to decide what level of risk you can live with, and whether or not to incorporate is the right choice for you.

TAKE ADVANTAGE OF BEING FEMALE

Not in the way you might think. Register as a HUB, DBE, WO, or MB/WBE. Say what? Many cities, states, and other entities offer certification to minorities and women as underutilized or disadvantaged businesses. This designation can take many forms, including a Historically Underutilized Business (HUB), Disadvantaged Business Enterprise (DBE), Woman-Owned (WO) Business, or Minority Business/Woman Business Enterprise (MB/WBE). See the Appendix for a list of certifying agencies.

The HUB program was created to remedy a disparity that existed in awarding contracting opportunities to minority and woman-owned businesses. For instance, I know a woman who used to be a surveyor. Now, surveying is primarily a male-dominated field. She was just as qualified (perhaps more so!) than any male surveyor in her peer group, but nine times out of ten, when listed side by side with a male surveyor in the phone book, customers would call the male surveyor to do the job. HUB status provides an incentive for the customer to call the female surveyor.

The HUB program provides a method to track how much business is done with minorities and women. Most state, federal, and other agencies are required to make a good faith effort to include HUBs in bid opportunities, which is judged by the total percentage of HUB contracts awarded. HUB certification increases your exposure to solicitations for the procurement of goods and services by these agencies.

The advantage to obtaining a HUB designation is that, as a woman, not only do you receive access to these bid opportunities, but your company receives special emphasis when bidding on government contracts. In some cases, businesses listed in HUB databases are used exclusively by companies when sending out bids.

Other companies may want to partner with you because you are a HUB (thus bringing in new business you would not have had before). If you are good at what you do, and the state (or other government entity) can comply with HUB laws by securing the services of a competent contractor (you!), then this is a "win-win" situation for everyone involved.

SEP IRA

As a self-employed individual, you need to set aside money for retirement. There is no company-sponsored 401(k) plan available to you. One way to do this is through a Self-Employed Individual Retirement Account (SEP IRA). SEPs serve as a tax shelter by allowing a certain percentage of your annual income to be put aside for retirement. SEPs have an advantage over traditional IRAs, in that the amount of money you can contribute to a SEP is much greater. Contact your CPA to find out more information about IRA options that are right for you.

STARTING A BUSINESS CHECKLIST

1. Develop a business plan. Include what products or services you are going to offer.
2. Set up an office – either at home or elsewhere (see Chapter 16).
3. Determine your business name and structure. File the appropriate paperwork, including an assumed name certificate if you decide to be a sole proprietor.
4. Open a business banking account.
5. Purchase office supplies, including business cards and stationery.
6. Transfer to your husband's health insurance policy (if applicable).
7. Register as a HUB or Woman-Owned Business.
8. Fill out IRS SS-4 Form to obtain an Employee Identification Number (EIN).
9. Apply for a sales tax and/or reseller certificate through your state comptroller office.
10. Keep track of all business expenses.
11. Open a SEP-IRA.

EXIT STRATEGY

By the time you set up your business, file paperwork, and build a client base, you have invested a substantial amount of time, money, energy, and effort into your business. Once you're in this position, especially if you have existing, ongoing clients, it will be difficult for you to quit and go back to work for someone else. Your clients will have come to rely and depend on you. Have you thought about how you will transition out of your business when you're ready to move on?

Rather than leaving your clients stranded, one recommendation is to find another consultant or instructor to refer your business to. Another suggestion is to take your projects with you if you go back to work for another company. These projects will be added value that you bring with you, so that may be an incentive for your new employer to finish them up. Hopefully, once you get started, you will want to be out on your own for a long time, but it is always a good idea to have an eye toward the future, especially when it's your own.

CHAPTER 3

Cynthia Long
Project Manager

In 1997, at the age of thirty five, Cynthia Long quit a stable, secure job in state government to open her own consulting business. With a background in Information Technology (IT) and Management Information Systems (MIS), Cynthia achieved immediate recognition and distinction as a consultant. Today she works part time as a consultant and as a full-time mom to her young daughter.

After twelve years of working for others in the public and private sector, Cynthia Long decided to open a consulting business working for herself. With a degree in business analysis that launched her MIS career, Cynthia was more than qualified to go out on her own. In 1999, two years after starting her business, Cynthia became pregnant with her daughter, Sarah.

Cynthia talks about making the decision to go solo, and how working part time afforded her the flexibility she needed with a newborn daughter. "I was tired of working for other people, and I wanted to be in business for myself. I wanted to be the hired gun that people brought in from out-of-town, that everybody listened to. I was able to take off nine months after I had my daughter (now four years old, at the time of this writing). For me, working part time is cyclical, where I may work on a project for several months, then I won't work for several months. It has always been like that, rather than working part time as in 20 hours a week."

Cynthia's expertise implementing large software applications, managing projects, and integrating systems gives her a broad range of skills that are in demand by many companies, regardless of the industry. One of her first customers was a company that manufactured engines, a seemingly unlikely candidate for an IT project. Cynthia served as the project manager for installation of a new Enterprise Resource Planning (ERP) system; a large, integrated software package containing financial, inventory, and manufacturing modules (e.g., SAP software).

Designed to increase efficiency, ERP systems allow companies to get more organized, have data in a common location, track assets, and share information between departments. Cynthia also made recommendations for computer security measures and supervised a team who put together the company's e-commerce website.

She obtained the business through a contact that she had met several years prior. The man remembered her, and called her when he needed to hire subcontractors to work for him on the project. Cynthia's experience reminds us of two things: that networking is crucial to those who are self-employed, and how important it is to meet the decision makers on a project.

She elaborates, "Traditional marketing doesn't work as much as networking for independent consultants. On any assignment, I always made an attempt to meet people within the organization who have influence selecting consultants in the future. I also try to hook up with other consultants. As an independent consultant, most of the time you are going to subcontract to a prime contractor, which is actually a better deal. It frees me up to do the job, instead of worrying about politics, bureaucracy, and paperwork. If you do a good job for the person who hired you, they will hire you again. One man who contracted for different companies kept calling me every time he moved to a new company, so I got the business."

After that first job, Cynthia's business snowballed. She worked on subsequently larger projects, including some in Europe, and Central and South America. She says that travel is a necessary evil, but she limits how long she is gone.

"Be willing to travel. It is essential, especially if you live in a smaller metropolitan area. You must go to the company's headquarters, where decisions are made (vs. a regional office). When you have children, it is more difficult to travel. When my daughter was born, my husband and I agreed that one of us should be home with her. When I am gone, he is there, and vice-versa. She is our only child and you only get one shot at doing it right."

Cynthia believes that contracting with a lot of different companies gave her experience that she wouldn't have had otherwise. "By working for myself, I had a lot of different experiences in many different industries. When you work for one company, you don't get that. For the first five years I was in business, I worked for an electrical components company, an airline, an engine manufacturing company, and an international conglomerate. I was able to gain firsthand experience and see all aspects of all those different businesses."

One of the toughest and scariest moments when starting out on your own is going from a steady paycheck to suddenly having no income. Planning for this situation ahead of time can help ease those fears. One recommendation is to save as much money as possible before starting a business.

Cynthia comments on her "lean" years. "Before I started the business, my husband and I saved as much money as we could. We had enough to live on for one year. When I left my full-time job at the state, I had a one month contract. As it turned out, the project lasted 18 months, but I never had more than a one month contract at a time. Some people can not handle that. My personality is high-risk, so it didn't bother me. If I started the business and six months later fell on my face, we wouldn't lose the house. We live frugally – we still live in the first house we ever bought, and I drive a 1986 Honda, which is the same car I had in college. My philosophy is that as you begin to make more money, increase your standard of giving, not your standard of living."

A real "go-getter," and a firm believer in community service, Cynthia served as a City Council member, and even ran for state representative. Cynthia talks about her tendency to spend too much time on extracurricular activities, "One of the hardest things for me to learn was to limit my outside commitments. When I first started out, I was on City Council. I lost a lot of income by giving up what could've been billable hours to the City Council. In hindsight, I don't think doing civic work and starting a new business are a good mix. You have to choose. When you're just starting out, you have to spend more time on your business."

Cynthia offers some advice to other women who are just starting out on their own. She says, "If you are married, you must have the support of your spouse and family. Going out on your own is a risk, and it can be a financial drain. It is also a lot of hard work at first, but it is worth it. A friend of mine asked his 90-year-old grandmother what she would've done differently in life. She said 'Take more risks.' I agree, and I would add that the hard work and 'start-up' phase of a new business makes us tougher overall. You tend to learn more about yourself (strength of character) during tough times, rather than when things are easy."

For Cynthia Long, working part time gives her the flexibility she needs to spend time with her family. It works for her because she and her husband make a concerted effort to ensure that one of them is home with their daughter at all times. Her business is not only financially rewarding, but also keeps her mind active, which is a nice benefit in addition to keeping her family happy.

Many thanks to Cynthia Long, my friend, colleague, and fellow commissioner, for participating in this project. Cynthia can be reached by email at clong@columbus-group.net

CHAPTER 4

Selling Yourself

Selling yourself and your services is one of the most difficult aspects of going out on your own. In fact, the number one reason many self-employed people end up going back to work for someone else is that they simply could not successfully sell their product or service and/or keep business coming in the door.

Marketing yourself and getting the word out about your services is critical if you are going to succeed. All self-employed people must do sales, at least initially. There is no getting around it.

NETWORKING

Call, call, call. Many of the women profiled in the case studies called everybody they knew when they first started out (and I did too!). Calling someone for advice and/or to share information frequently leads to referrals and additional contacts. It's important to let people know what you are doing! Even if you don't like the idea of picking up the phone and "cold calling" someone you don't know, do it anyway (if you don't know what to say, use the sample script in Chapter 1). It gets easier with practice.

One of the most effective sales techniques is networking. To borrow a slogan from a popular cruise line, "Get out there!" (and get connected). Make contacts within your industry. Find professional organizations in your field, and make an effort to attend and be seen. Volunteering for a leadership position will increase your visibility and exposure. Once you start going on a regular basis, you build rapport with other members through regular and periodic contact.

There are many groups that exist simply to promote networking and help make business contacts. I attend a bi-monthly college alumni breakfast dedicated to business-to-business networking. There are also networking organizations specifically for women – some local groups, as well as a national group called Women in Technology (For more information on W.I.T.I., see the Appendix).

Be visible! In this case, the old saying "Out of sight, out of mind" certainly applies. People won't know to call you if they don't know you exist.

Research and attend association meetings, trade shows, and conferences in (and some outside of) your industry. People go to trade shows because they are looking for new ideas and solutions to their business needs. What a perfect opportunity to sell what you do!

Don't rent a booth (unless you can afford to) – that is an expensive option. Instead, submit an abstract and make a presentation at the conference as an attendee. When you register for the show, you will be given a badge and most likely a "Presenter" or "Speaker" ribbon for your nametag, which can be a great icebreaker and conversation starter when meeting new contacts at the conference. Everyone will want to know what you are presenting.

If you can't make a presentation or if the conference registration fee is too pricey, obtain a pass to the exhibit floor. Most conferences will provide this at no charge if you simply ask. Walk around and network with other people and companies in the vendor area. To start a conversation, you can say something like this:

> "Hi, I'm _____ (your name). I've never been to this type of conference before, and I'm trying to get a feel for what different companies in this industry do."

Then let the other person tell you what they do, and decide if it is a fit. If so, say,

> "Has your company ever thought about offering _____ (certified training, computer consulting, or whatever product or service you offer)? I'm looking for a company to partner with, and what I do could expand the services you offer to your clients."

This dialog will work especially well if the company doesn't have someone on their staff who provides the same services that you do. When you introduce yourself to other people, look them in the eye, and state your first and last name. It makes an impression. Make an effort to remember people's names – they will remember _you_ for having done so.

Don't get the idea that you can do everything over the phone or by e-mail. Some technical writers post their resumes on Internet sites such as monster.com, writingassist.com, or prospring.net. These websites act as virtual agents for organizations looking to hire writers who have specific skills (technical writing, or specialize in proposals, etc.). It's fine to post on these sites to supplement your marketing efforts, but don't underestimate the importance of "face-time."

There is no replacement or substitute for meeting people in person. Once at a trade show, I walked into a vendor booth. As it happened, the company was looking that very minute for a freelance writer to write an article for them. There I was! I immediately received an assignment that I otherwise would not have had.

BE LIKEABLE

To state the obvious, it helps to be likeable when selling yourself (and making presentations at conferences). How do you define likeable? Be nice, pleasant, approachable, flexible, optimistic, and genuinely concerned with other people's well-being. Make others feel comfortable.

SIX QUALITIES NECESSARY TO BE LIKEABLE
1. Pleasant demeanor.
2. Approachable.
3. Flexible.
4. Be optimistic and have a positive attitude.
5. Show concern for others.
6. Sense of humor.

One way to make others comfortable and to be likeable is to employ humor in everyday conversation. Another surefire technique is to be self-deprecating (employ humor that makes gentle fun of yourself). Don't criticize other people, and keep your problems and sad stories to yourself. Nothing turns people off faster than unloading your personal problems on them. In other words, make yourself be the kind of person that people *want* to do business with.

You can do several things to promote your business when you are not actively networking. Every business has slow periods; they are a natural part of the business cycle. Keep on working, even if you don't have billable work.

Use slow times to think of creative ways to promote yourself and your services. Write an article about your business (or volunteer to be interviewed) for your local newspaper. Write a column for a magazine in your field of expertise. Research bid opportunities and look for proposals and potential business online. (See the Appendix for more information.)

DIVERSIFY YOUR SERVICES, SKILLS, AND CLIENTS

Financial planners advise their clients to "diversify their portfolio." My version of this advice is "diversify your client base." Take on clients from many different industries. I am fortunate because the GIS software I teach is used by many industries, including telecommunications, petroleum (oil, gas, and pipeline companies), school districts, state agencies, and municipal governments, among others. When you are self-employed, job security comes from having many clients (vs. working for the same company for 30 years).

In the same vein, it is also important to diversify your contacts within an organization. What will happen if your primary contact within an organization leaves or is laid off during a reorganization? Will your contract still be valid? Do you know someone else you can call?

This scenario happened to Ann Kasunich, a marketing professional profiled in Chapter 10. She explains, "I had a deal brewing with my former employer. It was a prearranged contract for marketing services they could give to their existing business partners. This would've been very lucrative for me if it had gone through."

She continues, "Unfortunately, my contact, who was the champion of the idea, left the company. Business relationships often start with one internal champion. Once that relationship is established, then you need to expand your connections to the organization and gain other allies. This is stronger position to work from, especially if one of your contacts leaves the organization."

In addition to diversifying your client base and contacts, diversify your skills, and the services you offer. For instance, I not only teach, but I also offer technical writing and consulting services. When I am not teaching, I spend my time writing articles, brochures, marketing pieces, and other items. I cross-sell my writing and consulting services to my existing students. How? By mentioning the fact that I am a technical writer during my classes, and also by e-mailing newsletters to them afterwards.

Another reason I stay busy is by offering classes from multiple software vendors, including competitors. Why not get the business, no matter what product the client buys?

TOP FIVE WAYS TO SELL YOURSELF AND YOUR SERVICES
1. Network.
2. Get referred (by doing a good job).
3. Take advantage of opportunities to market and self-promote your business.
4. Partner with companies who will sell your services for you.
5. Diversify your skills, services offered, and client base.

CLOSING THE SALE
When you talk to potential clients and you see that you are close to closing a deal, get in the habit of *asking* for the business. This is a skill that most women do not know to do. If you haven't already, ask your client, "What do you need?" Then tell them how your services can satisfy those needs: "I can help you by providing services _____ (A, B, and C)." (mirror what they told you). Then tell them you want the job, and ask, "When can we start?"

CREDIBILITY
Credibility is one of those intangible qualities that you can't buy, but it can make or break you. The same qualities that make you likeable make you credible. If you want to be likeable, do not criticize or badmouth other people. Gossiping or saying anything negative about anybody else can backfire and have the boomerang effect of damaging your own credibility.

Another basic rule is to look good. The concept of *face validity* is the belief that if it looks good, it *is* good. If you're going to stand up in front of a group and teach a class or give a presentation, people are going to be looking at you all day long. You will instantly be more credible, and therefore more believable, if you dress professionally and wear the best clothes you can afford (more on this in Chapter 14).

Establishing credibility may take time when you are starting out. It helps if you have a good reputation or are already well-known in your field. I had an advantage in that before I went out on my own, I worked for an industry leader in a sales job for two years. This high-visibility position gave me professional recognition and a network of contacts.

If you are just starting out and not initially well-known, consider giving presentations or seminars at professional conferences and trade shows. Not only will this expose you and your skills to a broad audience, but it also positions you as an expert in your field.

One thing that can help you establish credibility is to obtain any available certifications in your field (e.g., Microsoft® Certified Systems Engineer, or Certified Project Management Professional; see Chapters 6 and 11 for more information). Technical certifications give you a certain status, typically under a structured entity, recognized by others in your industry. These certifications can be listed on your business card as a marketing tool. Because you must be qualified to attain them, certifications provide instant credibility to potential customers.

A woman I know who is a Professional Certified Coach (PCC – see Chapter 8) maintains that certifications will differentiate you from others in your field who may not be qualified. Certifications will also put you on a qualifying list for jobs and bids. Frequently, government agencies and other entities will ask for a list of people who are certified, and then use that list as a pre-screener before hiring contractors and sending out bids.

Another way you can earn credibility and gain experience is by offering to do *pro bono* work for clients with a big name or a good reputation. These clients can then be listed on your resume as references. This strategy worked for Leita Hart, a CPA featured in Chapter 5. Leita also saved her course evaluations and showed those to potential clients, enabling her to obtain new business.

Tina Brown, a successful telecommunications consultant profiled in Chapter 7, offers some insight regarding credibility, "My own personal opinion is that you can't go into consulting while still in your early 20s.

You need time to build the expertise, as well as the respect of others in your field. Age and experience give you that advantage. When I train, I can talk about actual life experiences – building networks, and how I solved problems, etc. When you look at my course evaluations, at what people say, they always mention that I bring real-life experiences to the classroom."

FIVE WAYS TO ESTABLISH CREDIBILITY

1. Experience.
2. Reputation.
3. Certifications (if applicable).
4. Dress well.
5. Don't gossip!

GETTING BUSINESS REFERRED TO YOU

A client of mine once asked me about prospecting. "Karen, where do you get your leads?" I thought about the question a little bit, and then I realized that I really don't have to do that anymore; most of my business comes from referrals. In fact, I spend very little on advertising.

At some point in time, as long as you are good at what you do, then about 80% or more of your business should come from referrals. Realtors know this little secret – ask any realtor where most of their business comes from. Once you have built up a client base, ask your clients for repeat business and/or ask them to refer you (to companies they work with, friends, or colleagues). You may even consider offering your clients a small discount on their next project for each referral they give you that results in new work.

Obviously, referrals and networking are related. If you don't network, then you can't be referred. Develop and maintain your professional network. Face-to-face meetings are invaluable. They give you a chance to get to know the person, so he or she can see who you are and what you can do. First impressions are so much more memorable in person than over the phone. Don't call when you can meet someone face-to-face. And remember to be likeable!

Find companies in your field that will refer you and/or use or sell your services. Why would they do this? It benefits them because they can offer additional or expanded services for increased revenue without the expense of another employee.

I work with two companies that sell the software that I teach. One company is too small to maintain a full-time software instructor, so I teach classes for its clients as a subcontractor on an "as-needed" basis. The other company's sales representative passes out my business card and markets my services directly to his clients, and I pay them a referral fee when a job comes through. This gives both companies the advantage of being able to say they offer training without the expense of a full-time instructor. Obviously it benefits me because it is a source of income.

Another tip is to network with other consultants (even competitors) in your field. I have a colleague in another city who is also a GIS instructor. When she became overbooked, she asked me to teach some classes for her, which is business I wouldn't have had otherwise (and I was very grateful!).

WHAT TO CHARGE

I am always reluctant to discuss rates, because they vary so widely, depending on where you live and your professional specialty. If you absolutely have no idea what to charge, then use the following information as a guideline. What you charge depends on several things.

FIVE CRITERIA TO CONSIDER WHEN SETTING FEES

1. Cost of living and the going market rate in your part of the country.
2. What services you are providing.
3. The client's ability to pay.
4. Rates of competitors.
5. Your own profit margins.

First, remember that as a consultant, you bring value and experience to any situation, which justifies a higher fee. Don't feel guilty charging a high rate! Women often feel intimidated about money. Be confident. Keep in mind the advice from Chapter 1, that consultants are worthy of their rate and know it.

Another thing to realize is that when you go out on your own, you will probably not be billing for 40 hours a week. In fact, some weeks you may not have any billable work at all, which is why you need to charge higher rates. Cynthia Long, a computer project manager profiled in Chapter 3, says, "There are some places a consultant can't go. On the flip side, many times there is a place on a project for an individual consultant instead of a large corporation. You can always beat their rates."

Before you start out, research what the going market rate is for your services where you live. As stated previously, rates vary widely across the country, depending on cost of living in your area. At a bare minimum, most consultants charge at least $75 per hour, depending on experience. Some consultants charge a lot more. Ann Kasunich charges a minimum of $125 per hour for her marketing services, however, she has two factors in her favor. She is very well regarded in her field, and she lives in Southern California, where the cost of living is higher than in other parts of the country.

Rates vary depending on the service provided. A rate for training is different than one for consulting, coaching, writing, travel time, technical writing, or data entry. A starting rate for professional coaches is $75 per hour. Experienced coaches can make as much $125 or more per hour.

For writing, it's hard to beat the discussion on rates in Peter Bowerman's *The Well-Fed Writer* (Fanove Publishing, 2000). Writers can make anywhere from $50 to $125 per hour, depending on the task; fees for technical writers are a little lower, $35 to $75 per hour. Some writers charge by the article; fees can range from $500 to $1500 and up, depending on the length (see Chapter 9 for more on application articles). Writers who submit photographs with their articles can ask for more money.

A word here about travel time. Some consultants charge for their time to travel to and from a client site. If you decide to do this, I would not charge as high a rate as for the actual job. When I first started out, I bid on a proposal, and made the elementary mistake of bidding every task at the same rate. Because each task varied widely in skill level, I should have bid each task at different rates. Ultimately, I didn't get the job, and after that I learned to charge varying rates, depending on the service.

For training, most instructors charge by the class, rather than by the hour. If you provide onsite training, then giving your customer a group rate is a bargain. For example, if you teach a two-day class for $3500, which includes books and your travel expenses, and your customer has ten students, then that is $350 apiece for student tuition. Most "training centers" charge in the neighborhood of $850 or more per student for a two-day course and even more money for a three-day class. Use this fact as a selling point to your advantage, but be sure to limit the number of students to 10 or 12; any more than that is too much to handle for a single class.

Some instructors charge as much as $5000 or more for a two day class (still a bargain at $500 per student). Wouldn't it be great to make up to $5000 gross per month, working only a couple of days teaching a specialized class? Now imagine multiplying that number by three or four classes a month!

PROFIT MARGINS

Leita Hart, CPA and fellow instructor, talks about setting rates, "Decide what you need to live off of as a bare minimum. My very first contract gave me $20,000 per year, and, using that as a base, I built up my income. My first year, I made $30,000, and the most I ever made is $120,000 gross. I don't have one single client that gives me enough money to live on, but I have enough different clients to be able to earn a living. Today, I have seven steady clients who each give me $7000 annually. After that, the rest is gravy."

Jenny Harrison, another instructor profiled in Chapter 12, compares her income now to what she was making previously, when she had a full-time job at a consulting firm. "Now that I'm out on my own, I do make a little more gross income than when I was employed full-time. However, if you factor in the benefits (health insurance, etc.) the company was paying for me, then the amount is probably equal. Don't work part time if you think it's going to be easy or that you're going to get rich."

BE COMPETITIVE

Be competitive by scouting out your competitors' rates. You can find information online, or better yet, if you know any people in your field, just come right out and ask them what they charge (tell them you are conducting research). If your client has a lot of work for you to do (i.e., 40 hours per week or more), offer them a volume discount on your rates. The bottom line is to provide outstanding service for a reasonable fee, which keeps your clients happy and gives them good value for their money.

GETTING PAID

Are you prepared to deal with clients who don't pay you what you're owed? As a business owner, one of your top priorities should be getting paid for your services. This is a reality of being in business for yourself: You have to collect your own payment by submitting an invoice (a fancy term for a bill) to your clients. (A sample invoice can be found in the Program Files, Microsoft Office, Templates directory).

"People are funny about money" is a universal truth, no matter what business you are in. Believe it or not, but some of your clients may not want to pay you, even after you have satisfactorily completed the work. Generally speaking, if you do business with large, reputable corporations, and/or government agencies, they will pay you. It may take 30, 60, or even 90 days to receive payment, but eventually you will get paid.

I can honestly say that I am very lucky, in that all my invoices have been paid. I always make sure I have a signed contract, letter of agreement, or purchase order as a backup, in case there is ever a dispute. What is that?

A purchase order, or P.O., is a document that an organization issues to you ahead of time for the services you are going to provide. When you invoice the organization, put the P.O. number on the invoice. If the organization you are doing business with does not work off of a purchase order system, ask for a signed letter of agreement on their letterhead, stating the services you are going to provide and the dates. The other option is to submit the letter on your stationery and have them sign it.

If you're having trouble getting paid for a job, get creative. If you have to, camp out in the company's waiting room or lobby and don't leave until you have a check in your hands. For more good ideas on getting paid promptly, read Chapter 9 of case study Leita Hart's book, *The Four Principles of Happy Cash Flow* (Fanta Sea Publishing, 2004).

Once, I was having trouble with a company that wouldn't pay their invoice. Every time I called the president of the company (who had attended my class), his secretary took a message and my call was never returned. I finally called early one morning at 7:00 A.M. The president's secretary wasn't in yet, and he answered the phone himself. I explained that I had been trying to contact him for weeks, and that my invoice hadn't been paid. When confronted in person over the phone, he sounded rather sheepish, but the check was sent out that same day.

One way to avoid these hassles and get paid immediately is to accept credit cards. When you take a credit card, the entire amount is immediately deposited into your account, and you pay a fee to the bank (usually a percentage of the sale) for the transaction. Today, even government agencies commonly pay with a credit card, rather than issuing a check, so it is a good idea to investigate this option.

In short, you may have to "get tough" when it comes to collecting payment, but it is hoped that these times will be few and far between.

WHAT IF THE CLIENT CAN'T AFFORD TO PAY YOUR GOING RATE FOR THE JOB?

This is a different situation than not getting paid by the client. If you're in a meeting with the client and they are non-committal, it may be that they want to hire you but can't afford your services. In this case, ask your client what the budget is for the project. You'd be surprised at how open most are with that information.

Be flexible. Adjust your rates according to the client's budget, and 90% of the time you will get the business. I know one graphic artist who never quotes a set rate. Instead, he adapts the level of his work to whatever the client's budget is, no matter how big or small the job.

This is a smart way to do business, because it provides him with a constant stream of work and income – from projects ranging from $100 to $50,000. Lesson learned? Sometimes it's better to have paid work at a lower rate, than no work at all!

CHAPTER 5

Leita Hart
Certified Public Accountant

I magine a CPA who doesn't like paperwork! Leita Hart decided to go out on her own more than nine years ago. Now she teaches classes in financial management, budgeting, and auditing to other CPAs, universities, and private corporations.

As a CPA herself, Leita had instant credibility, and developed her own course materials to teach classes to a specialized market. In 2002, Leita had her first child. Today she continues to be a successful business woman while working part time and staying home with her daughter.

After graduating from the University of Texas in Austin with an accounting degree, Leita Hart went to work for a CPA firm. She found she did not like accounting work, and changed jobs, going to work in the public sector as an auditor for the Texas State Auditors Office (SAO). While there, she was asked to put on training seminars, which is how she started teaching classes. After working as an auditor for a while, Leita decided to try her hand once again in the private sector, working as a comptroller.

It was at this point that Leita made the decision to change her life and go out on her own. According to Leita, "My first job at the CPA firm did not jazz me whatsoever. After my stint at the SAO, I decided that I did not like accounting or auditing. I decided to try one more job as a comptroller, and that was the worst one out of the three. I knew I had to do something drastic to change my life. I was also in a bad marriage at the time, and I was simply miserable. I decided that I was going to quit working and start a business. My first husband and I were married during the first two years, the start-up phase, of my business, although we divorced two years later. I have been doing training ever since."

When Leita started out on her own in 1995, she called everybody she knew to see if they needed training. She also did some work "on the side" for some prestigious clients while she was still employed full time. Leita comments, "I started doing free work for the Texas Society of CPAs, as well as the State Auditors Office (her former employer) before I quit my job. If you have those clients on your resume, it looks good. Those clients lent me their name, not their money."

She continues, "I also called everybody I knew, including companies who sent me catalogs. One company (Bell Learning Systems) responded, and gave me a chance. One class I taught for them turned into a year-long contract. I also joined various professional organizations, including the National Speakers Association, and the American Society of Training and Development, where I received a lead to teach at Dell Computer. In my business, course evaluations are a big deal, and my ratings are high. I kept those evaluations and showed them to potential clients. Don't get me wrong, I do have bad days – everyone does. When I first started out, I had more bad days than good. It took a while to perfect my presentation. But over time the word spread and I built up my business."

Today, Leita is self-employed and teaches many different accounting courses to a host of different clients. She has written several books and more than 20 seminars, and can customize each seminar to fit the needs of any customer. When the client is a university, Leita teaches classes in understanding financial statements, budgeting, and government accounting. When the audience is other CPAs, she offers classes on balanced scorecard management, financial statement analysis, and auditing topics. She also teaches business writing, and finance for non-financial managers at large corporations. Most of her classes are only one day long, and she usually teaches two days each week.

Leita talks about buying pre-developed course materials versus developing her own. "If you purchase canned materials, it can easily cost thousands of dollars. If you are knowledgeable about your topic, it's fairly easy to write your own materials. I have had experience both ways. Once, I used another instructor's materials, which were weak, and I ended up having to supplement them with my own anyway. There were also mistakes in some of the slides. Much to my chagrin, one student in the class challenged everything I said and pointed out all the mistakes aloud, in front of the other students. That is a very difficult situation to be in when you are trying to teach a class. I had to defend these materials that I hadn't written, so after that I developed my own."

Leita talks about customizing course materials for clients, and emphasizes to research the market beforehand. "First, I found out what the client would buy, and then I created it. Don't do it the other way around! Course development can take anywhere from four to six weeks, and you don't want to waste your time. Do the market research first, and let the client tell you what they want. Then decide whether or not you can develop it. This has always worked for me."

Leita doesn't sell any of her course materials to other CPAs or instructors. Her reasoning is that she would feel responsible for the quality of the course, if taught by someone other than herself. Most instructors understand this.

In 2001, Leita remarried, and had her first child in 2002. Now 37 years old, she reflects about the decision to reshape her life, "I planned to only work part time. I set a goal to only work two days each week, teaching classes. Sometimes I have to travel to and from the client site, which makes for a longer work week."

When asked about working from home, Leita says, "Usually my daughter is home with me, but she stays with a neighbor a few hours each afternoon, so that I can get other work done. This year, my husband quit his job to start his own business. It has been difficult, but now we both have much more flexible schedules and can spend quality time with our daughter. We alternate staying home with her. Now that I am married to the right man, we share the responsibilities of raising our children. It is a wonderful feeling and makes a world of difference to my happiness."

As of this writing, with her daughter just over two years old, Leita and her husband are now expecting their second child. Leita comments on trying to teach when pregnant, "Well, obviously it's tiring. Typically, I am a high energy trainer. I am all over the room. When I'm pregnant, I conducted the class sitting down the entire time. What's surprising is that the course evaluations were the same. I found out that CPAs didn't like me walking around all over the place. I also try to hide my moods from my students. If you're professional, you can do that."

Leita offers some advice to other women who are just starting out on their own. "Pick something and stick with it. When I discovered that I hated accounting, I wanted to abandon my investment in my education and do something else entirely. My Dad coached me to stick with something – he's 57, and very successful. When things get hard, it's easy to want to drop it, but I have stuck with it. There have been times when it's been very hard, and I didn't like my work. I didn't like some clients, so I chose not to renew with them. For cash flow purposes, sometimes you have to keep clients you don't like until someone else replaces them."

When asked about having the motivation to make a life change (for more on this, see Chapter 1), Leita has this to say, "People will not change unless God whacks you upside the head. For me, things were so miserable that I didn't have a choice. I talked about it for years, but I didn't want to leap off the cliff. A girlfriend of mine works full time and misses being home, but I really don't think she will make a change unless something drastic happens, for example if she is laid off. If you don't act after a while, then God will intervene, and you will get what you want. However, it may not be in the pleasant manner that you were expecting. Have faith, but you also have to help make it happen. Another thing I can say is write down your goals. That has been very effective for me."

Leita continues to build up her business through creative marketing efforts. She says that a universal truth for all sole proprietors is that you have to be good at what you do. Early on, she developed a relationship with a university professor who continually refers her, and that has added up to a lot of business through the years. She has also recently begun emailing a monthly electronic newsletter (e-zine) to all of her clients. The newsletter contains "how to" tips, rather than information about Leita. As a result, she is already booked up for most of the coming year. Now that's job security!

Leita Hart's conscious restructuring of her life has paid off in big ways. She says, "I am very happy with my life now. Working part time has really served me well, especially now that I have a family."

She adds that there were a lot of things about the corporate world that she does not miss, including the commute, non-flexible work hours, meetings, and bureaucracy. Leita says she will never go back to that world again.

Fortunately, she doesn't have to.

Many thanks to Leita Hart.
Leita is the author of the upcoming *Accounting Demystified* and *The Four Principles of Happy Cash Flow*, available at www.happycashflow.com.

You can find out more about Leita at
www.leitahart.com
or email her at Leita@leitahart.com.

CHAPTER 6

Freelance Consulting or Working Part Time in your Field of Expertise

This chapter, in addition to Chapters 8, 9, 11 and 13 are designed to provide options and ideas for part-time and flexible careers you can start from home. There are several factors that make part-time employment feasible for women in a wide variety of fields, especially those who work with computers.

In today's high-tech world, an increasing number of women are computer literate and/or experienced in computers, computer networking, programming, and systems administration. In general, more women hold college degrees today than at any previous time in human history.

I have a colleague who is a successful contract computer programmer. She specializes in several programming languages, including Visual Basic, VBA (Visual Basic for Applications), and various scripting languages (custom languages written for specific software programs). She works with a lot of high-tech companies, building computer software and applications for those companies and their customers. One day almost two years ago, she approached me for advice about going out on her own, and she has been going strong ever since.

If you know any programming languages, then you have a very marketable skill. Nevertheless, part-time and flexible career options are certainly not limited to the computer field. The ideas, strategies, and techniques found in this book can be applied to almost any industry or field.

Think about what you do for a living. Is it something that you can do part time out on your own? Working part time can apply to almost anyone, in any field: graphic artists, meeting planners, salespeople, proofreaders, real estate agents, editors, nurses, physical therapists, financial planners, mortgage brokers, Web developers, database and network designers, massage therapists, even lawyers. The case studies in this book are CPAs, project managers, technical people, instructors, consultants, and marketing professionals. I know one hair stylist who only worked on Saturdays after having kids.

Use your imagination. The possibilities are endless! Whatever you decide to do, plan for it now in order to make it happen.

WORKING PART TIME FOR SOMEONE ELSE

Why not approach your employer first about the option to work part time? Have you thought about this? The worst he/she can do is say "no," and he/she might even surprise you by saying yes. If you can switch over to your husband's health insurance policy, then your employer saves money by not having to pay benefits for a part-time employee. Your current employer already knows you, what you're capable of, and how hard you are willing to work, so it's worth a shot.

Look at Maria Shriver. After she had her first child, she approached her employer, NBC, about working only part time in her capacity as an on-air anchor. Because she had already established herself before having kids, her boss knew how hard she worked and agreed to her proposal. After that, she was able to anchor at least two hour-long news specials each year. She has continued to work part time in television for more than ten years.

Another example is a woman I know in the healthcare field. Anne is a physical therapist who works part time (as needed) for a local hospital. She has two daughters, six and eight years old. At the time her oldest was born, Anne quit her full-time job at the hospital and took ten months off to stay home with her daughter.

When Anne was ready to go back to work, she went back to work as a contractor one day each week. After a while, the hospital hired her back as a part-time staff member at the same salary she was earning as a contractor. Once her daughters were older and in school, she increased her hours each week, but still works less in the summer in order to stay home when her kids are out of school.

By transitioning to part-time employment as a physical therapist, Anne is able to maintain her career while caring for her daughters. She can work part time because she sees only patients who are newly admitted to the hospital. The fact that she is not the primary therapist limits the amount of time she spends with each patient, as she doesn't have to follow patients throughout their entire hospital stay. Recently, Anne has begun to add home healthcare visits to her workload, as her schedule permits. She provides physical therapy to in-home patients once a week, for an hour at a time.

If your employer is not open to letting you work part time, then you may want to consider the next step – going out on your own. Many people who go out on their own start out by contracting back to their previous employers. The advantage is that your current employer already knows you and the quality of work you do, so it is a natural fit.

WHAT IF YOU DON'T LIKE WHAT YOU DO?

You are not alone. Many women find that once they have obtained a professional degree, they do not like the day-to-day work involved in the profession. For some reason, this seems to be true for many accountants and lawyers. Fortunately there are other options.

If you have a professional occupation, perhaps there is something slightly different within or related to that profession that you can do, using your expertise. For example, two lawyers I know conduct seminars in their respective specialties (employment law and elder law), rather than actually practice law. They give workshops to corporations, other lawyers, and specialty groups. Other lawyers provide jury consulting services.

Leita Hart, a CPA profiled in Chapter 5, discovered she didn't like accounting work after trying her hand at several jobs after graduation. Acting on the advice of her father, who told her to "stick with it," Leita decided to stay in the accounting field. Today, she teaches classes and workshops in financial management, budgeting, and auditing to other CPAs, universities, and private corporations. Another option is to consider buying a franchise business (more on this later in the chapter).

TECHNICAL CERTIFICATIONS

Are there any technical certifications (also called "designations") you can obtain in your field? Certifications are programs offered through various high-tech manufacturers, software companies, and other entities that allow qualified professionals to attain a certain status recognized throughout an industry. This "seal of approval" is a valuable marketing tool, which can be listed on your business card, website, or other marketing pieces to provide you with instant credibility to potential customers. This is especially helpful if you are not yet established or well-known in your field.

By design, certifications are not necessarily easy to obtain. Many have stringent requirements, including a certain number of years of work and/or project experience, a difficult exam, and demonstrated proficiency in a software or technology via presentation or a "hands-on" test. Once you have been accepted into a certification program, typically you will pay an annual fee to the manufacturer to maintain the certification.

Having technical certifications can often justify charging higher rates than you could without them. Other benefits you may receive from the manufacturer can include a free copy of the software after you pass the exam and pay the certification fee, use of their corporate logo (on your business card or letterhead, for example), and discounts on future training, merchandise, classes, or other purchases.

Certifications can be used for teaching and/or for consulting purposes. What follows is a partial list of available technical certifications. (For teaching certifications, see Chapter 11.)

CERTIFIED FINANCIAL PLANNER (CFP^{TM})

With the demise of corporate pension plans and social security not so "secure," many people are finding themselves responsible for their own financial future and retirement income. If you have a background or a degree in accounting or finance, you might consider becoming a Certified Financial Planner.

CFPs provide professional advice and guidance to people who want to grow their money and investments. The CFP designation differentiates financial planners from the growing multitudes of people calling themselves "financial advisors." CFPs demonstrate their competency by passing a stringent exam, and meeting additional requirements for experience and education.

MORTGAGE BROKERS

Another option for those with a finance or accounting degree, is to become a licensed mortgage broker. This turned out to be the perfect career choice for my friend Angela Anders, married with a one-year-old son.

Having no prior experience in the industry (she ran hotels for a living beforehand), now she makes a good income working out of her house.

Angela's husband is a real-estate agent, and together, they set up their own home-based business, Anders Realty & Mortgage Group, Inc., using each other's complementary skills. He shows houses while she secures the financing and loans for the buyers and sellers. She and her husband alternate work hours so that one of them takes care of their son at home while the other is working.

Angela has the flexibility to work when she wants to, and can be with her son during the day. She says, "When it is a nice sunny day, I love having the freedom to put my son in a stroller and take a walk down to the park. I am so fortunate in this regard. After my son goes to bed at night, I can then sneak back into the office and make up the work I missed during the day."

To become a mortgage broker, you must apprentice as a loan officer after passing a state exam. After becoming a loan officer, you must be sponsored by a licensed mortgage broker for a period of 18 months before you can apply for a broker's license. A mortgage broker license is required before you can do business with lenders. Check with your state government for specific requirements.

PROJECT MANAGEMENT PROFESSIONAL

Project managers are professionals who supervise all aspects of a project. Project managers exist in any industry, and their duties include serving as the primary point of contact for all subcontractors and other staff working on the project. They also provide technical guidance, review invoices and specifications, determine quality control and other procedures, inspect data, and maintain schedules and budgets. Overall, they are responsible for making sure that all work connected to a specific project is completed. (For a project management case study, see Chapter 3, Cynthia Long).

The Project Management Institute (PMI) is the world's leading not-for-profit project management professional association. If your educational background or area of expertise is in project management, you may want to consider obtaining a professional certification as a Project Management Professional (PMP) from PMI.

One benefit to obtaining a PMP certification is that the designation is widely recognized by large corporations and other organizations. They know they are getting a professional who has a certain amount of project management experience and education, and who adheres to standardized policies and procedures. (For more information, please go to www.pmi.org. All links herein subject to change.)

CISCO® CERTIFICATIONS

Some project managers have a specialized area of expertise. Tina Brown, a Cisco Certified Network Professional and a Cisco Certified Design Associate profiled in Chapter 7, specializes in designing and installing infrastructure for LAN (Local Area Network) and computer networks. Cisco Systems, Inc., founded in Silicon Valley in 1984, is the worldwide leader in computer communication networks.

Cisco has certifications available to competent professionals who demonstrate proficiency and expertise in four different areas of Cisco networks: Network Engineering and Design, Network Installation and Support, Network Security, and Service Providers. Within each certification area there are three increasing levels of demonstrated proficiency: Associate, Professional, and Expert. (Please note that the information provided herein is only for general informational purposes; please go to www.cisco.com for more information and for specific certification requirements.)

CCDA®, CCNA®

The Associate designation within the Network Engineering and Design category is the CCDA, or Cisco Certified Design Associate. CCDA certified professionals can design routed and switched network infrastructures involving LAN, WAN (Wide Area Network), and dial access services for businesses and organizations. The Associate designation within the Network Installation and Support category is the CCNA, or Cisco Certified Network Associate. CCNA certified professionals can install, configure, and operate LAN, WAN, and dial access services for small networks (100 nodes or fewer), including but not limited to use of these protocols: IP, IGRP, Serial, Frame Relay, IP RIP, VLANs, RIP, Ethernet, and Access Lists.

CCDP®, CCNP®, CCSP™, CCIP™

A Professional designation, one level up from the Associate designation, indicates advanced knowledge of network design. Within the Network

Engineering and Design category, a Cisco Certified Design Professional (CCDP) can design routed and switched networks involving LAN, WAN, and dial access services, applying modular design practices and making sure the entire solution adheres to the business and technical needs of the client.

Network Installation and Support is for professionals who install and support Cisco technology-based networks in which LAN and WAN routers and switches reside. The Associate designation within the Network Installation and Support category is the Cisco Certified Network Professional, or CCNP. Professionals with a CCNP designation can install, configure, and troubleshoot local and wide-area networks for enterprise organizations with networks ranging from 100 to more than 500 nodes.

Computer security is a growing concern for many companies. Contractors with expertise in computer security systems are sought after and well-paid. Cisco offers the Cisco Certified Security Professional, or CCSP, within the Network Security category. CCSP professionals can design, build, and implement complete end-to-end security solutions, including manage network infrastructures.

The last Associate designation is the Cisco Certified Internetwork Professional, or CCIP, found in the Service Provider category. CCIP professionals have detailed understanding of networking technologies in the service provider arena including IP routing, IP QoS, BGP, and MPLS.

CCIE®

A Cisco Certified Internetwork Expert certification is the top level of any Cisco category, indicating extremely specialized knowledge and expertise of Cisco networks. The "Expert" status is available in three categories: Network Installation and Support, Network Security, and Service Provider.

CCIE certification in Routing and Switching, the most popular CCIE track, indicates expert-level knowledge of WAN, LAN and dial access networking across a variety of routers and switches. CCIE certification in the Security track indicates expert-level knowledge of the configuration and maintenance of secure enterprise networks. CCIE certification in the Service Provider track indicates expert level knowledge in at least one of the networking areas specific to service provider environments. These areas include Dial, Cable, DSL, Optical, WAN Switching and IP Telephony.

CISSP

If your background is in computer security, but your knowledge and expertise is more broad (i.e. not focused on a particular manufacturer, software, or brand), you can apply for a Certified Information Systems Security Professional (CISSP) designation. Many places offer training and classes for the CISSP exam. Computer security professionals control access to a company's computer systems, both internally and externally; and oversee development and installation of software applications, cryptography, operations and physical security, and telecommunications, network, and Internet security. (For more information, please go to www.cissp.com.)

COMPTIA

Computing Technology Industry Association, or CompTIA, is an association of more than 8000 companies in the IT industry. CompTIA provides computer certifications for IT professionals in a variety of subjects, including A+, Network+, Server+, I-Net+, Linux+ (Note: There is also a separate designation for Linux System Administrator certification), Security+, and many others. CompTIA offers a fairly new certification for professionals in the document imaging/management industry called the CDIA (Certified Document Imaging Architech)™. (For more information, please go to www.comptia.org.)

NOVELL

Novell was one of the first companies to offer commercial networking software and information technology (IT) solutions. Today, in addition to networking services, Novell offers Linux support, Web services and application integration, and cross-platform computer networking.

Novell offers certifications in several key areas, including consulting, sales, technical support, and educational services. Some of the Novell certifications available are: Certified Novell Administrator, Certified Novell Engineer, Certified Linux Engineer, Master Certified Novell Engineer, and Certified Novell Salesperson. (Please go to www.novell.com for more information and specific certification requirements.)

ORACLE®

The first company to commercialize the relational database model for businesses, today Oracle is one of the largest software companies in the world. Oracle has expanded on its origins to deploy 100 percent Internet-enabled enterprise software across its entire product line: databases, business applications, and application development and decision support tools. Oracle offers three categories for certification as an Oracle Certified Professional (OCP): Database Administrator, Application Developer, and Web Application Server Administrator. (For more specific information regarding each certification, please go to www.oracle.com.)

SUN MICROSYSTEMS™

Founded in 1982, Sun Microsystems originally manufactured UNIX workstations. The company then pioneered TCP/IP computer network protocols for the Internet. Through the years, Sun released the Solaris operating system and Java, the first portable universal software platform. Sun offers several certifications, including Java Technology, Application and Directory Servers, the Solaris Operating System, and Network Storage. (Please go to http://training.sun.com/US/certification/ for specific information regarding each certification. Note: All links subject to change.)

MICROSOFT® TECHNICAL CERTIFICATIONS

Microsoft Corporation is one of the most recognized names in the computer industry. Microsoft develops and manufactures all types of software and operating systems, from the popular MS Office Suite (which, depending on the edition, includes Word, Excel, Outlook®, Publisher, Powerpoint® and the Access Database programs) to MS Windows®. There are several certifications available from Microsoft. (For a complete list and specific requirements please go to www.microsoft.com.)

- MCP, or Microsoft Certified Professional. The MCP credential is for professionals who have the skills to successfully implement a Microsoft product or technology as part of a business solution within an organization.
- MCSA, or Microsoft Certified Systems Administrator. Duties include administering network and systems environments based on the Windows platforms.

- MCSE, or Microsoft Certified Systems Engineer. Duties include analyzing business requirements to design and implement an infrastructure solution based on the Windows platform and Microsoft Servers software.
- MCDBA, or Microsoft Certified Database Administrator. The MCDBA designs, implements, and administers Microsoft SQL (Structured Query Language) Server™ databases.
- MCAD, or Microsoft Certified Application Developer. The MCAD use Microsoft technologies to develop and maintain department-level applications, components, Web or desktop clients, or back-end data services.
- MCSD, or Microsoft Certified Solution Developer. The MCSD designs and develops leading-edge business solutions with Microsoft development tools, technologies, platforms, and the Windows architecture.
- MCDST, or Microsoft Certified Desktop Support Technician. The MCDST supports users and troubleshoots Windows desktop operating systems.
- Microsoft Office Specialists are globally recognized for demonstrating advanced skills with Microsoft desktop software.

OTHER CERTIFICATIONS

There are literally hundreds of certifications available from software manufacturers and other organizations. Some certifications demonstrate proficiency in software, such as Lotus® Notes from IBM® (www.ibm.com/certify) and Oracle, while others signify achievement within a profession, such as knowledge or project management, or a Webmaster (CIW, or Certified Internet Webmaster). (For more information on Knowledge Management Professionals, go to www.eknowledgecenter.com.) Professionals who work in Human Resources (HR) have their own certifications. (See www.shrm.org and www.hrci.org).

Only the more well-known certifications are listed here. You can conduct your own research for certifications in your field or area of expertise. Ultimately, it will be up to you to decide which certifications are worthwhile. Consider your return on investment. Is there sufficient demand for those services that you will be able to quickly recover the cost of the certification fee?

CONSULTING

If you have an expertise, specialized skill, or market niche, then consider working as a consultant. Consultants are needed in almost every industry. Your knowledge is valuable and will allow you to make a nice living.

In today's information-based society, companies will pay for someone else's information, knowledge, and experience, especially if it saves them time and money. Consultants have the flexibility to set their own schedules, frequently are not required to do the work on-site, and don't always have to have a backup if they need to take a day off.

Karen Strong is a perfect example of someone who works part-time in her field of expertise. (For additional consulting case studies, see Chapters 3, 7, and 15). Karen is an industry recognized consultant, speaker, and author in Enterprise Content Management, or ECM.

Originally born in the late 1980s, when paper documents were scanned onto microfilm, the industry evolved due to the introduction of electronic documents and document scanning technology. Today ECM technologies capture, manage, store, preserve, and deliver content and documents related to organizational processes. The "content" in ECM includes Office Suite software such as word processing documents, spreadsheets, and presentations as well as scanned images, Web content, database files, and e-mail messages.

Karen started in the industry 22 years ago, right out of college, and has grown with the industry. She has an undergraduate degree in business plus an MBA (Master's in Business Administration). She holds two certifications in her field – an MIT (Master of Information Technology) and an LIT (Laureate of Information Technology) from the leading industry trade association (AIIM International) based on her specific ECM industry expertise and experience.

At first, she worked for two different industry vendors and traveled extensively. After literally becoming physically exhausted from traveling, she made the decision to go solo in 1991. Karen comments, "I left the corporate vendor world to do independent consulting. At the time, I was on the verge of getting married, and I wanted to control my own destiny and not travel so much. Plus, working for a vendor, I was selling solutions to clients that weren't necessarily in their best interest. As an independent consultant, now I am not associated with a vendor, and I am free to make more appropriate recommendations to my clients."

Today, Karen has a son and a daughter, ages eight and nine. She consciously structures her day around her children's school schedules. She only works when they are in school, starting work after 8:00 A.M., and leaves in the early afternoon so she can pick them up. After school time is allocated to children's activities, homework, PTA, and other "mom" activities. Then when the kids go to bed, e-mails are answered and client projects completed.

Karen says that when she is on-site at a client's office, other women see her come and go, and wish they could do the same. "A lot of women that I work with are moms too. They sit behind a desk from 8:00 A.M. to 5:00 P.M. every day, and would give anything to do what I am doing. What they don't know is how hard I worked to achieve the flexibility that I have. My clients tease me when 3:00 P.M. rolls around – they say 'There she goes, signing off, she's a mom now.' Fortunately most of my clients have kids of their own and understand and appreciate why I leave early."

Karen is another example of a professional who built up her business and then scaled back to part-time once she had children. She says, "I won't travel. I used to attend and speak every year at the AIIM International Conference, which is the major conference for my industry. I would come back with so many leads but then I wouldn't pursue the business because of the travel required. After a while my husband asked me, 'Why do you even bother to go if you don't take on the work?', so now I don't go to the conference anymore."

Karen talks about how she handles consulting opportunities that she ends up turning down. "I tell the client I can do high level strategic planning instead of the daily work required on-site. I will do light travel where I may have to be gone overnight, but then I will subcontract out the rest. I am set up as a corporation (Clarity Inc.) specifically so I can prime contracts. Otherwise I say 'I am not the right person for you.' Then I try to find someone else I can refer to take on the work – preferably someone that gives a referral fee."

WHAT IF YOU DON'T HAVE A SPECIFIC SPECIALTY?

Don't despair if all of the certifications listed in this chapter seem overwhelming or don't apply to you. I know a woman who started out by simply enrolling as a student in a basic Novell class. She picked it up very quickly, and in no time at all, she became certified as a Novell instructor and started teaching classes out on her own.

Another thing to consider is that a bachelor's or master's degree, regardless of what field it's in, or a professional designation such as a CPA (Certified Public Accountant) or P.E. (Professional Engineer) already gives you credibility to go out on your own, so you may not need a certification.

FRANCHISES

Another option you may want to consider is purchasing a franchise. There are many businesses available through franchises, including Computer MOMs (see Appendix for more information). Mentors On the Move (MOMs), is a home-based business specializing in providing one-on-one computer training at the client's home or place of business.

Other franchises can be purchased in almost any field or area of expertise, including leadership development, Dale Carnegie training (communication skills and interpersonal techniques), and financial services and investment. There are also many retail franchise opportunities. If you don't like the idea of purchasing a franchise outright, you might consider contracting as an instructor or seminar leader for one of these organizations (i.e. CareerTrack® or Fred Pryor Leadership Development seminars).

One of the many advantages of purchasing a franchise business is instant credibility through your association with the parent company. Another is having access to "ready-made" course materials, market analysis, shared marketing and advertising costs, and, in some cases, a start-up client list.

Buying a franchise may allow you to discover a hidden strength in a new area, which might be one way to deal with burnout. (For more tips on dealing with burnout, see Chapter 14.) For Celia Thompkins, a CPA who switched careers, purchasing a franchise allowed her to develop and grow in a new direction professionally. (See Chapters 11 and 17 for Celia's comments.)

At any rate, with so many opportunities available, you are bound to find something you can do part-time. Chapters 8, 9, 11, and 13 present additional part-time career options, including professional coaching, freelance writing, teaching software classes, and public speaking.

CHAPTER 7

Tina Brown
Telecommunications Expert

In 2003, Tina Brown left a high-level position as Vice President of a nationally known telecommunications consulting and training firm to go out on her own. By combining her unique background in telecommunications and adult education, Tina has now built a successful part-time consulting and training business.

Today Tina not only teaches classes in telecommunications, but she can also design and install data networks, and manage large network implementation projects. Married with one son, she recently decided to reprioritize her life by placing her family first. This chapter tells the story of Tina's journey.

Tina Brown grew up in a small town south of Houston, Texas, along the Gulf Coast. After high school, she started college at the University of Houston, but ended up joining the military after only one semester. Little did she know that the experience she gained in the Navy would pave the way for the rest of her career.

While in the Navy, Tina served as a Radioman School Instructor, where she developed curriculum for Navy communications courses. After that she served onboard the USS Dixon, based in San Diego, where she was responsible for shipboard communications. All told, Tina served on active duty in the U.S. Navy for 11 years, and eventually retired from the Naval Reserves.

Along the way, she took college courses wherever she could, and in 1987, Tina graduated with an undergraduate degree in adult education.

Two years later, she completed an MBA with an emphasis in telecommunications. By merging her education and her telecommunications background, Tina was able to lay the foundation for her eventual part-time employment.

After her Navy career, Tina went to work for a consulting firm in San Diego. During this time, there was a downturn in the economy, and Tina was laid off. Tina describes her situation this way, "I worked as a software tester for one year, and then there was a downturn in the defense industry. I knew I was going to get laid off because the company assets were being sold off, which is not a good feeling. It was a wake up call for us on the vulnerability of the job market."

She continues, "My husband and I decided our lifestyle should be based on a single income, and because of the cost of living, that we needed to leave San Diego. We both began to look for jobs outside of California. I found a job working for the (Texas) Department of Information Resources (DIR) as a communications specialist in Austin, Texas."

After moving back to Texas, Tina continued to gain technical experience in telecommunications, computer networks, and network routing. She can install computer networks, manage installation teams, and has expertise in TCP/IP, local area network (LAN) protocols, routing protocols, and Cisco communications hardware and software. Tina has professional certifications as a Cisco Certified Network Professional and a Cisco Certified Design Associate (see Chapter 6 for more information on Cisco certifications). She is the co-author of *Data Network Design* (ISBN: 0-07-219312-3), published by McGraw-Hill/Osborne in 2002.

After she left the DIR, Tina was recruited to work for a telecommunications company that was just getting started into the network management business. She provided network engineering support to domestic and international customers. This support included consultation, technical design, proposals, installation, and management of customer wide area networks.

At this point, Tina left her full-time job and briefly went to work on the Alaska Pipeline as a contractor, where she quickly realized the financial benefits of contract work. While in Alaska, Tina worked through a prime contractor, Spohn & Associates, who eventually hired her as a Vice President after the project was complete. Spohn & Associates specializes in providing corporate network management, including WAN (Wide Area

Network), LAN (Local Area Network), Wireless, and Information Security consulting and training services. Tina worked at Spohn for three years before leaving to go out on her own in 2003.

While most people would find the thought of leaving a good position at a nationally known company just a little bit scary, Tina wasn't nervous about leaving. "When I went to Alaska, I knew that the pipeline project was only for four months. I was hoping that the project would be extended, but overall I was excited more than I was scared. When I left Spohn, I was not afraid. I carefully planned my exit and was prepared financially. I also left on great terms with the CEO who offered me contract work immediately."

One thing that can be terrifying for women is "jumping ship" (so to speak) and leaving a secure well paying job to go out on their own. Planning for this situation ahead of time can help ease those terrors. One thing that many people do is secure contract employment through their current employer prior to leaving. In Tina's case, she still does a lot of contract training for Spohn & Associates, her former employer.

Another prepatory step that can be done before leaving that steady paycheck behind is to save money. Tina offers some advice, "I had saved enough money financially so I could be unemployed for up to two years. My husband and I decided that since I was going to go out on my own, that we needed to have at least two years worth of salary in the bank. I was also very fortunate in that one company I worked for went public. On top of that, we saved a significant sum of money the year we lived in Alaska. Those two things allowed me to pay off my home. Once I didn't have a mortgage payment, I had the financial security and freedom to go out on my own."

For Tina, deciding to make a change and work part time was a major life adjustment. Tina's hectic schedule and long hours contributed to her decision. She reflects on her decision, "Last year I decided that I was working too much and was not spending enough time with my family. If I had to do it over again, I would've done this years earlier. I used to work 12 to 16 hours a day, and that limited the time I spent with my family. I decided that it wasn't too late and knew it was time for a change."

Not long ago Tina secured a contract with a company working every other week as a Chief Technology Officer. She elaborates, "This contract is an awesome opportunity for me. It combines strategic thinking with day-to-day management decisions related to technology. Because I am away from my family two weeks out of the month, I am very committed to limiting the amount of travel I do in the remaining two weeks. Now, when I am home, my family has my full attention. It is great!"

Since leaving her full-time job, Tina is able to "pick-and-choose" the jobs she works on. She not only teaches telecommunications classes, but also develops curriculum for many of the courses. In addition, she manages computer and communications networks for a wide variety of companies.

Tina comments on consciously making the switch to part-time work, "My history has been to take on more than I can do. Now I turn work down. I don't have the desire at this time to hire employees and build a business. I work with a group of consultant friends that I respect and can call on. I give them the work, and in turn, I know that they will call on me when they get work."

Tina touches on one very important aspect of self-employment – networking. Professional networking is critical to any business. Many times it's who you know, not what you know, that will get your foot in the door for a job.

Tina secured her current part-time contract through a personal contact. She says, "The first thing to do is to build relationships within your industry, which provides a foundation. Don't expect it to happen overnight. All of the contracts I am currently working on came from professional contacts I made years ago. I meet people on airplanes, join professional organizations, ask people to lunch, etc."

Tina talks about how important it is to gain credibility when working for yourself, "First, you have to gain respect in your field. That takes building both relationships and credibility. I have been successful because I am ethical. I see so many things that are unethical in my business. Those who are unethical – it will come back to haunt them. Most of the people I work with now, I worked with in the past. People knew me and knew my work ethic, and knew I would give 100%. One company called me for a job because they knew I had a good reputation."

Tina believes her work ethic came from her years in the Navy. She says, "I felt I had to work harder than the men in order to be equal. Women were less than ten percent of the military population and were not allowed in combat roles at the time. Working hard was the only way to compete for better jobs."

Tina offers some advice to other women who are thinking about going out on their own and working part time; "Be flexible. A guy called me the other day looking for a job. He wanted to make $250,000 per year. In a down economy, that is simply not realistic, especially when so many are unemployed. You need to adapt when the industry changes. One other thing I can say is don't concentrate on the negative. Remember the positive aspect and appreciate what people do for you, and what opportunities are presented to you. Appreciate and build relationships."

For Tina Brown, transitioning to part-time work has been one of the best changes she has ever made in her life. She is able to spend more time with her family and focus on only the jobs that she truly wants to do. By her own admission, the only regret she has is that she didn't do it sooner.

Many thanks to Tina Brown,
Owner and President
RWJ Enterprises
tina@rwjenterprises.com

CHAPTER 8

Professional Coaching

Professional coaching is a relatively young and still evolving profession. Coaches have a lot of flexibility because they can work when and where they want to. Coaching sessions can be done individually in-person, on the telephone, or through group sessions. A coach can limit the number of clients she takes on, in order to work part time. Generally, coaches charge by the hour, or offer phone packages which include a certain number of coaching sessions for a set fee (for specifics on rates, see Chapter 4).

HISTORY OF COACHING

The idea of coaching as a profession started to become popular in the mid to late 1970s, after former tennis champion Timothy Gallwey wrote *The Inner Game of Tennis* (Random House, 1974). Gallwey's book presented the unique and radical idea that an athlete's body had the innate ability to perform by itself. The role of an athletic coach, meanwhile, was to ask questions that increased the athlete's awareness of how they were playing and then let the athlete adjust his or her performance accordingly.

At the time, Gallwey's methods were a departure from the traditional role of an athletic coach as someone who offers constructive criticism and calls strategies. Many of those who read *The Inner Game of Tennis* were executives. These business people realized that the ideas presented within the book could be applied to the corporate work world, and moreover, that coaching within a sport could be applied to everyday life. The concept of business and corporate coaching stemmed from this realization.

Similarly, present day coaches believe their clients are already creative and resourceful, and the role of a coach is to listen and guide their clients to draw solutions and strategies from within themselves. Rather than telling you what to do and giving you advice, a coach helps you discover your own answers to situations or problems and supports you while you implement them. The goal of the coach is to help their clients take steps to address areas of specific change the clients have identified in their lives.

WHO USES A COACH?

Today, many individuals hire a coach in order to receive direction, feedback, and guidance specific to their situation and life goals. Similar to mentoring, coaching is a form of business partnering that many times results in ongoing long term relationships between the client and coach. Consultants, on the other hand, come in as experts, and bring the answers in, while coaches take the time to help their clients find the answers.

In the last decade, coaches have become a popular resource, especially for entrepreneurs, business people, and even other coaches. Many motivated individuals and professionals hire coaches. People who need coaches range from self-employed sole proprietors and independent consultants, to executives or other professionals (attorneys, physicians, and even other coaches) and government employees, supervisors, and leaders.

Other people who uses coaches are those looking to get ahead or reach that "next level" in their career or business. They may need some extra mentoring or coaching in order to reach their goal. All types of professional salespeople, from stockbrokers, bankers, insurance agents, and realtors may hire coaches to help them achieve their next big sales goal or quota. Other candidates for a coach are parents, athletes, teachers and professors, corporate managers, and creative types – writers, artists, or philosophers.

CATEGORIES OF COACHING

Coaches are in-demand more than ever before. In general, people are more aware of coaching as a profession, and also more accepting of what coaches have to offer. In today's world it is not uncommon for someone to hire a specialty coach who can help them with all aspects of life, including spiritual growth, parenting issues, exercise, and nutrition, in addition to business and career decisions. There are also generalist coaches who have a broad range of experience.

Life coaches are known to guide people to find direction in their lives, make decisions, create structure, or restructure/reexamine options during a transition. Life coaches can help clients reduce stress, achieve goals, commit to an exercise routine, and get organized. A life coach with a relationship specialty can help clients through relationship issues and achieve personal growth as a human being.

Career coaches guide individuals, entrepreneurs, and sole proprietors to make key changes to develop or help grow their business and improve or change their careers. Technology coaches work with companies to find new markets, redesign or reevaluate existing products, and innovate new ones. Technology coaches are visionaries, having the ability to think and see at least ten years into the future.

Corporate coaches may specialize in developmental tools to build key skills to various levels of staff within a company. A corporate coach may specialize in increasing employee motivation and satisfaction, and, as a result, staff retention. (High staff turnover can be costly to companies if they have to keep training new employees.) Corporate coaches may also offer techniques to improve leadership skills and interpersonal communications.

Parenting coaches are specially trained to help parents work through issues and make appropriate decisions regarding their children. Coaches help parents with common problems including how to control the influence of TV and the media on their children, behavior problems, conquering each childhood "stage," and building a child's self-esteem. Coaches use positive reinforcement and motivational techniques, among others, to help parents accomplish their goals.

WHAT DOES IT TAKE TO BE A COACH?

First and foremost, you must have or develop excellent communication and people interaction skills. The coach listens and then shares his or her honest feedback with the client, in such a way that the client is heard and not made to feel wrong. A coach must be a quick study, in order to understand where their clients are in life, and be able to recognize their individual skills, talents, and strengths.

Coaches draw from their own personal life experience to offer insight and direction to their clients. Women, in particular, are especially adept at sharing their knowledge with others. Although age does not necessarily go hand-in-hand with experience, age gives you a certain credibility when dealing with people. Experience also comes from professional and life experience, career advancement, and personal growth.

Coaches blend their background with their unique life experience, and the essence of who they are as a person. Coaching is a very personalized profession, based on your own individual personality, expertise, focus, and style. Your clients must feel they can trust you, and be confident that that whatever they tell you remains confidential.

If you want to become a coach, you must be able to see things from all sides and offer a different perspective or viewpoint to your clients. Coaches help their clients find their way or niche in life. Ultimately, coaching can be a rewarding profession, as coaches see their clients grow and develop as a result of their influence and guidance.

KEY FACTORS NECESSARY TO BE AN EFFECTIVE COACH

1. Excellent communication skills.
2. Trust.
3. Ability to listen.
4. Be able to draw from your own unique life and professional experience.
5. Ability to recognize a client's individual skills, talents, and strengths.
6. Ability to see a situation from all perspectives.

WHO ARE COACHES?

Coaches come from all walks of life. Many Certified Financial Planners, or CFPs, (see Chapter 6) and Certified Public Accountants (CPAs) serve as default personal financial coaches to their clientele. Many people have changed careers to become a coach; some had long distinguished careers in other professions. The skills and techniques learned in other professions can be used to complement coaching skills.

Coaching is perfect for former career women who quit working in order to stay home and raise their kids for a few years, and are now looking to rejoin the working world. People regularly hire coaches these days for all kinds of things, including parenting. If you're a mom looking to go back to work, why not put your wisdom and experience back to work as a coach?

COACHING CERTIFICATIONS

In Chapter 6, we learned that certifications provide increased credibility as you become established in your field. Obtaining a professional coaching certification is a way to distinguish yourself from other people who do not have any formal coaching training. There are several avenues to certification as a coach.

The International Coach Federation (ICF) is the primary body that represents and supports professional coaches. To become a certified coach through the ICF, you must first graduate from an Accredited Coach Training Program (ACTP). Flexible classes, designed to work with and around your schedule, range from a period of weeks, weekends, or months, depending on the provider. For a list of current ACTPs, go to www.coach-federation.org (Note: All links subject to change). The ICF program is tiered, meaning that you must obtain a lower level certification first, before you can apply for a higher-level certification.

Generally speaking, to obtain a coaching certification candidates must take required training courses and coach a minimum number of clients. The lowest level of ICF certification is an Associate Certified Coach (ACC). An ACC is an apprentice coach who has received 60 hours of coach specific training and who has already coached a minimum number of clients. The next level is the Professional Certified Coach (PCC), and the top level is the Master Certified Coach (MCC), requiring significantly more hours of training and experience. An MCC signifies an elite status among coaches.

There are other organizations that support certification through the ICF. Coach University (AKA Coach U) offers training programs that qualify for the ICF ACC, PCC, and MCC coaching designations. (See www.coachinc.com for detailed information). The Coaches Training Institute also offers programs that count towards ICF certification (See www.thecoaches.com. Note: All links subject to change).

Most coaches recommend becoming certified if you want to be a coach. Because the ICF is a structured entity that represents the coaching profession, becoming certified as a coach through the ICF differentiates you from someone else who hangs out a shingle and calls themselves a coach.

The good news for moms who are looking to rejoin the workforce is that the requirements for obtaining a coaching certification are straightforward. Once you are prepared, trained and ready, use the techniques found elsewhere in this book to market yourself, sell your services, and build up a client base.

CHAPTER 9

Freelance Writing

I f consulting or coaching doesn't appeal to you, then how about writing? Most people picture writers as some sort of starving artist, ekeing out a living writing articles or books. However, there is an entire other realm to freelance writing that most people do not know about.

What is it? Corporate writing.

Due to two corporate economic trends over the past decade, outsourcing and downsizing (layoffs), corporations have effectively scaled back their in-house marketing, communications, and graphics departments. Outsourcing means that these companies regularly hire freelancers to do their writing work.

What kind of writing work? Marketing brochures, flyers, annual reports, advertisements, newsletters, direct mail pieces, press releases, business letters, sales and promotional materials, proposals, etc. According to Peter Bowerman, author of *The Well-Fed Writer* (Fanove, 2000) and a successful freelance commercial writer in Atlanta for over ten years, there is virtually unlimited demand for this kind of copywriting work, especially in large metropolitan areas.

Many books (including Bowerman's) have been written that teach you not only how to write but also how to sell your writing services, so I am not going to try and duplicate that information here. In contrast, this chapter is designed to provide you with some ideas on where to start, who to approach, and what to write.

As a standard disclaimer here, let me say that this chapter also assumes that you have some kind of innate writing ability. Freelance writing is not for everyone. Like anything else, writing skills are developed and honed over time. The more you write, the better at it you become.

WHAT'S YOUR AREA OF EXPERTISE?

It's always a good idea to leverage what you know, no matter what your specific field. Whether you are in banking or finance, insurance, real estate, high-tech, healthcare, or something else, you have an advantage over other writers in that you are an expert in that field. You know the issues facing that industry, which adds value to your writing.

Use your network of contacts, people you know, to offer writing services to companies in your field. When I started out, I approached several GIS (Geographic Information System) and GPS (Global Positioning System) companies about writing application articles and user stories. Build up your client base first, and then eventually you can begin to write for other clients outside your field.

If you have a background in sales, use your knowledge to craft and strategically position an ad, brochure, product, article, or even a company. Your sales experience can add a persuasive sales tone to your writing. Find out the features of the product or service you are writing about and highlight the benefits they bring to the customer. Your goal when writing is to bring about a result, which can mean anything from motivating the potential customer to pick up the phone and call the company for more information, to actually buying the product.

WHO DO YOU CALL?

In addition to calling contacts from your own database, research who the marketing managers are at companies (consulting firms, non-profit organizations, accounting firms, software companies, insurance companies, hospitals, hardware manufacturers, and high-tech companies – all have writing needs) and call them. You can get names from company websites or from industry trade magazines.

Look at the trade magazine advertisements and read the articles. Which companies advertise and/or are mentioned in the articles? It's a pretty good bet that they used a freelancer to write the article.

Another place to get names are industry directories. Some are free for the asking, some are not. In addition, some industry magazines regularly publish a directory of their product vendors and advertisers. Peruse these lists to seek out new clients.

APPLICATION ARTICLES

Application articles are a great way to get started writing. Almost all companies have some user or customer success story they would like to profile or feature in a magazine. And not all application articles end up in magazines – they can be used on websites and as other marketing or promotional materials. Freelance writers are hired to get the message out. The idea is that once prospective customers see how others are successfully using the company's product or service, then they will want to use it too.

I once wrote an article for a major consulting firm about a project they did in Arkansas. The firm had developed a project management system that tracked facilities, assets, and ongoing construction projects throughout all Arkansas state parks. After the article was published, the consulting firm received a call from the park system in another state that had read the article. Ironically, the other state was facing the same situation (managing assets) and asked the consulting company to bid on the job. That's the idea behind application articles – to get the word out and increase sales as a result.

Companies use application articles as a marketing tool. Usually it costs less for them to hire you to interview their happy customers and write an application article for a magazine than it does to place a full-page ad in the same magazine. Plus, they get more exposure, because most articles are more than one page long. Because magazines do not typically charge to run articles (and are even grateful to get the content), companies receive more exposure and publicity for less money than placing an advertisement.

Use this fact as a selling point to your advantage when you approach companies. First, research how much it costs to place a full-page ad, then adjust your rates so they are lower. Here's a pitch you can use when calling marketing managers:

> "Hello. My name is _____. I am a freelance writer specializing in _____ (finance, healthcare, insurance, etc.). Have you used writers in the past to write application articles for you?" If the answer is yes, state what

you can write and your rates, "For $500 less than it costs you to run a full-page ad, I can write you a three page application article to be placed in _____ magazine."

TRADE MAGAZINES

Research trade magazines in your field. What are trade magazines? Not usually available (or interesting) to the general public, these are magazines that specialize in knowledge and information specific to an industry.

The subscribers tend to be professionals in that field, whatever it is. (Some examples of trade magazines are *Government Technology*, *Transmission & Distribution* for the power/electrical industry, *Coal Age* for the mining industry, and *Bank Technology News* for the financial/banking industry. Others can be found listed on http://industryclick.com/icmagazines.asp, www.freetradepubs.com, and www.business-marketing.com. (Note: All links subject to change). Many vendors have their own in-house magazines they send out to their customers.

Call the magazine and introduce yourself to the editor. Say:

> "Hi, my name is _____. I am a freelance writer, and I am familiar with your magazine. I can write articles on _____(finance, healthcare, insurance, etc.), which would fit in your upcoming issue. Do you pay writers for their articles?"

If the answer is no, then ask for the names of companies who regularly advertise in the magazine (they may need someone to write the ad) or who use freelancers to write application articles. Many times, the magazines themselves are looking for freelance writers, or have clients who are, and will either hire you or refer you. Remember to ask for the business (see Chapter 4). Because the magazines are so specialized, there are usually fewer writers vying to place an article in a trade magazine than in a national magazine. (Note: You can try submitting proposals to mainstream magazines, but unless you are a well-known author, the competition to land an article in a national magazine is extremely fierce.)

While you're at it, request a copy of the magazine's editorial calendar. Most magazines feature certain topics for certain months (themed issues).

This allows you to call prospects or clients ahead of time and alert them to an upcoming issue on a topic relevant to their business, where they may want to feature a piece (and have you write it!). The editorial calendar also allows you to keep abreast of deadlines, as articles are usually due two or three months before the monthly issue is actually printed.

TECHNICAL WRITING

Another avenue to explore is technical writing. This is a broad term that can refer to anything from product documentation, software manuals, user and reference guides, product specification sheets, "white papers" (technical product or software articles), to standard operating procedures (SOPs). In my field, I have written many GIS/GPS software and hardware manuals, as well as product specification sheets and SOPs.

Given the current tendency of corporations to outsource writing projects, technical writers who specialize in this kind of work can suddenly find themselves in high demand. In addition, many freelance writers don't care for technical writing, so if you have a technical proficiency or expertise in a certain field, it can be very lucrative. (For a discussion on rates, see Chapter 4, "Selling Yourself.")

COURSE DEVELOPMENT

Software instructors and trainers (see Chapter 11) have an advantage over other writers, in that they can write course materials. If you have been teaching a course for a long time, you should know what can be done to improve it. Companies often hire outside instructors to re-write their courses when the courses change due to new software releases or for other reasons.

MARKETING/COPY WRITING

As the old saying goes, "You can build a better mousetrap . . . but nobody will buy it without any marketing or advertising." Companies must spread the word about their product or service to get people to buy it. When you think about how many marketing messages you are bombarded with every day, from TV to radio to the Internet, it is truly mind boggling. Like it or not, marketing is a necessary evil in our society.

Many smaller companies and even large ones do not have the staff, resources, time, or talent to create brochures or write marketing copy about their product, business, or company. That's where you come in. Small software companies or other businesses may have a fantastic product or service, but if nobody knows about it, they probably aren't selling much of it.

Your job is to find these companies and offer copywriting services to them. (For a detailed marketing communications case study see Chapter 10.) If you do a good job for a company on one piece, it can lead to other work. There are all kinds of marketing material you can write: corporate brochures and image pieces, advertisements, website content, newsletters, direct mail pieces, corporate profiles, annual reports, proposals, sales letters, success stories, user profiles, application articles – you get the idea.

OFFER DESIGN SERVICES TOO

It helps to team up with a graphic artist. For the same reasons that companies don't do their writing in-house, chances are they don't do any graphic work in-house.

I have worked with a graphic designer for several years now, in order to offer "one-stop-shopping" to my clients. This means that clients can come to me to get their marketing pieces written and designed all in one place, which gives me an advantage over other writers. I serve as the coordinator and sole point of contact, and my client sees only the finished product – a slick eye-catching marketing piece that they absolutely love!

TRAVEL WRITING

If there's one area of freelance writing that most people jump at, this is it. Can you imagine getting paid for your dream vacation? It can happen. There is one catch: for this job, travel *is* required.

There are three main areas of travel writing: articles, guides, and books. Travel articles are by far the largest market. There are magazines devoted exclusively to travel, while others feature a travel section or one travel article per month. "Lists" (Top Ten Summer Fun Destinations, etc.) and "how-to" articles are very popular, but be sure to identify the readership and market for each magazine before submitting a query.

Travel guides are written for a specific destination; examples are Frommer's and Michelin. Travel books can fall into two categories: literature or an author's memoir or personal travel account. (*Italy Fever* by Darlene

Marwitz is an example of the latter.) True-life travel tales often pay the most money, provided they're dramatic enough.

Obviously, one of the main benefits of travel writing is actually getting to go to the destination you are writing about. Another benefit is getting paid to go and/or writing off the cost of your trips on your income taxes. I worked briefly as a travel writer for a local magazine. Typically, my assignments were "day trips" – places to hike, explore, shop, and dine around Central Texas.

During that time, my husband and I went on a fabulous three-week vacation to Italy. When I got back, the magazine I wrote for asked me to write about our trip for the next issue. Whoopee! My $3000 Italian vacation just became a tax write-off. On top of that, my husband, a very good amateur photographer, took the most beautiful photographs on our trip. The magazine paid him to use the photos, which meant we were able to write off both of our trips that year.

Make no mistake about it, competition for travel writing is intense. Match your ideas with the results of your market research for each magazine you query. Again, it helps to write about what you know, so if you have specialized knowledge, don't hesitate to use it. This is one way to differentiate yourself from other travel writers, and from other writers, period.

Travel articles must inform, entertain, educate and persuade, while also creating a unique sense of place. They should generate attention, interest, desire and action, hopefully in the form of reservations on the part of the reader. When writing a query letter, keep in mind that the goal of the editor is to sell the publication.

IF NOT WRITING, HOW ABOUT EDITING?

Not everyone is a natural-born writer. If writing is not exactly your thing, but you are good at grammar and proofreading, then why not try your hand as a freelance editor? There is a lot of demand in the writing community for this service.

Take Mim Eisenberg, of WordCraft Inc., in Roswell, Georgia, a suburb of Atlanta. Mim worked as an office administrator for 30 years before moving to Atlanta in 1994. Fifteen months later, and three weeks after moving into her new house, she was laid off. It was then that Mim, who had always had a knack for proofreading and editing, and who had already been doing transcribing part time, decided to turn her supplemental income into her primary profession, and WordCraft was born.

Today, Mim offers tape transcription services for oral historians and personal historians, plus editing, proofreading, and administrative support. Her clients are located nationwide, and Mim has the flexibility to set her own hours. She says, "Starting WordCraft was the best thing that could have happened to me. I wouldn't trade this for anything."

SUMMARY

So, as you can see, there is both a wide variety and range of corporate, technical, marketing, and other writing work out there. How much work you take on, and how much time you devote to writing, is entirely up to you. It's your job to seek it out and turn it into a part-time income!

CHAPTER 10

Ann L. Kasunich
Marketing Professional

For ten years, Ann Kasunich worked for a leading software manufacturer in Southern California. While there, she worked in several different areas of the company, including corporate and product marketing, proposal writing, and sales. Her work experience, combined with an MBA, provided her with a good foundation for going out on her own. In 2001, Ann started her own home-based marketing communications and consulting business.

Two years earlier, in 1999, at the age of 33, Ann found out she was pregnant with her son. Immediately she approached her boss about the possibility of more flexible working conditions. In her case, she wanted to work out of her house in order to stay home with her infant son a few days each week.

Initially, the company agreed, and allowed Ann to work from home. She was able to do writing work (news releases, Web content, demo CDs, and internal communications) at home, while still attending meetings at the office. The arrangement worked very well for Ann until two years later when a corporate policy change pulled the rug out from under her.

It was at this time that Ann made the decision to quit her job. She talks about her decision, "When the policy changed, they wouldn't let anybody work from home, so I decided to quit. I realized that I had to start my own business because I need to work, financially and personally. In fact, I don't know how NOT to work."

She continues, "On my last day, I lingered at the office . . . I really didn't want to leave. After I finally left, I drove straight to Office Depot and purchased blank business stationery. When I got home, I printed 'ALK

Consulting Group' on the letterhead. At this point, I had written many business plans, but I didn't have a plan for me!" Laughing, she continues, "Today, I tell all my clients to plan, but I didn't do it before I went out on my own, and I certainly wouldn't recommend that to anyone else."

Starting out, Ann and her husband, Tom, were prepared to make financial sacrifices. According to Ann, "After I quit, we figured out how much we needed each month. For the first three months, by supplementing what we had with our savings, we broke even. We cut back on everything. It's amazing what you can cut when you look for it."

Faced with a hefty mortgage payment, dwindling savings, and no immediate income, Ann and Tom made the difficult decision to sell their home. Ann recalls, "We called our real estate agent and put our house on the market. With our income cut in half after I quit, we had difficulty making the mortgage payments. Thankfully, the house didn't sell, and in that three month period of time, I made enough money that we could cover our expenses, including the mortgage. When I quit my job, I wasn't thinking about the house, I was thinking about our child. The house was less important to us than spending time with our son. We knew we could never get that time back."

Ann admits that everyone told her it would take at least six months to earn any money or land any clients. Turns out that wasn't true for Ann, who immediately took advantage of the existing network she had built over the past ten years. "To get started, I picked up the phone and called everybody I had known over the years. I was negotiating my first marketing contract a few hours later. I realized then that I should've quit three or four years sooner than I did."

Ann talks about getting started, and using her network to build up her business. "The fact that I worked for an industry leader gave me a lot of credibility. It means something to potential clients. I have a good reputation, and I take pride in my work. I still have contacts at my former employer who refer me. One lead came from a lady in advertising sales, she quit to go back to work for someone else and gave me all of her clients."

"Another company called me and said 'We heard you do great work. Can you help us?' I have had those clients and jobs for nearly two years now. At this point, I can decide who I want to take on and I am not as nervous about what's coming in next."

Today, Ann is still self-employed, providing marketing services to a host of clients. She writes articles, news releases, and marketing/business plans for clients, in addition to implementing those marketing plans, launching products, and developing content for websites. Most of her clients are small software companies whose technical staff doesn't completely understand the marketing world.

Ann develops a rollout plan to position those companies and their products in order to sell the software. Ann's objective is to have some kind of an action result from everything she writes. Her ultimate goal is to get buyers to call her clients and purchase their software and services.

Ann is fortunate, in that she doesn't have to travel to meet with her clients. Her former employer holds an annual conference in San Diego, which is only an hour and a half away from where she lives in Southern California. Many of the company's business partners and software resellers attend the conference. Ann can take advantage of this fact, and not only meet her current clients during the conference, but also look for new ones.

Ann is selective about her clients, and even turns down work at times. She explains, "I am very result oriented. When I work with a client, I make sure they get their money's worth. If they think they didn't get their money's worth, then they haven't advanced their company, and it could affect my reputation. Sometimes I need to help them refocus on their business goals and really consider the outcome they want before they hire me. This up-front focus on results is the foundation for my success and my clients' success. Those companies that are unable to articulate their desired outcomes either need to rethink their situation or hire me to help them figure it out before we move ahead on projects. Always consider the desired outcome before entering a contract, as it is better in the long run."

When asked what advice she would give to other women who want to go out on their own, Ann has a lot to say. "First and foremost, don't burn any bridges. Second, even if you don't have any billable work, keep full-time hours. When I first started out, I had an infant sleeping at my feet in my office, but I was available for my clients. I negotiated one of my first contracts late one afternoon on my cell phone, while sitting in the back seat of my car nursing my infant son. Once the deal was made, I got out of the car and finished the grocery shopping."

She continues, "Third, if you're going out on your own, it's easy to be scared. Try and look at it as a challenge. For me, it was very exciting, because I could build on my knowledge, but I knew I didn't know everything about running a business. You have two choices – stay where you are, or make the jump. If you fail, what's going to happen? Probably nothing – you won't be any worse off. Even if you don't get exactly where you planned at least you tried. Besides, so what? Just do something else. Fear can keep you trapped in a place you don't want to be."

Ann credits some of her outlook to being a competitive athlete while growing up. "Many female athletes don't have a fear of failure, or at least it is minimized. They have experienced competition, and winning and losing. Defeat at a championship game is a big loss, but when you wake up the next day you pick yourself up and life goes on. Once you understand life marches on after losing, it's not so scary. In fact, I believe that failure is really an opportunity to learn. If you look back and see where you went wrong, you can determine how to avoid that problem in the future."

Ann's decision to leave her job and pursue part-time employment has been rewarding, both professionally and personally. One unexpected benefit is renewed interest in her work. She says, "Immediately I discovered a renewed excitement for my industry. My clients are entrepreneurial and fun to work with. The companies that have the money to hire a consultant are generally healthy companies looking to grow to the next level of their business. It's very exciting to help them and be a part of their growth. When I was working for my former employer, at times I was unable to see that my work impacted their bottom line. On the personal front, I have lots of flexibility in my schedule. I am growing as a professional, while being available for my son."

Ann is grateful for the flexibility that self-employment provides. Ann's husband, Tom, has a flexible schedule and can also work from home. This creates a positive situation where they can alternate taking care of their son.

She elaborates, "I am busy every day from 6:00 A.M. to 10:00 P.M., but there's flexibility within those hours. I am able to not only work, but also take care of my son when he's sick, or chaperone on class field trips without worrying about whether my job is at risk. I still work very hard, but now I have freedom to create a schedule that meets the needs of our family. If I am on a tight deadline, my son visits with me for 10 or 15 minutes in my home office and then my husband comes to get him and they go somewhere else in the house to play. I wouldn't go back to a regular job, but I want people to understand that there's a balance to everything and as long as you're aware of that, I think it can all be managed."

Now that her son is older, Ann's business not only provides her with the freedom to set her own work hours, but more importantly, she is home every day when her son gets home from school.

She talks about some of the experiences she would've missed if she hadn't made the decision to leave her job and pursue self-employment. "I love it when my son runs up the stairs to my office screaming 'MOM! MOM! MOM!' He is so excited to tell me about his day. I wouldn't trade that for anything in the world. I have found that the neatest conversations and experiences with my son are spontaneous and at odd times during the day."

"I am so glad just to be around when he has thoughts he wants to share in the moment, or holding hands with him as we cross a street, knowing that someday very soon he won't need my hand. Or the time when we put a new comforter on my son's bed and the three of us laid on it together staring at the ceiling, talking and laughing . . . simple tender moments that make up life. I am thankful that I have skills that *allow* me to be there for those moments; otherwise we would all be missing out big time. I feel very connected to everything that is going on with my son's life in a very healthy way."

You can't put a price on that.

Many thanks to my good friend Ann Kasunich, whom I have known for more than ten years. Ann can be reached by email at:
ann@alkconsulting.com
or
www.alkconsulting.com

CHAPTER 11

Teaching Computer Software Classes

Have you ever attended a software class as a student, and came away feeling you knew as much as or more than the instructor did? If so, why not teach those classes yourself?

When initially confronted with the idea of teaching computer software classes for a living, for some reason most people groan and think, "I don't want to do that." However, you might be surprised, as many who originally are put-off by the thought of becoming an instructor, find that they not only enjoy it, but are even good at it! Moms are natural teachers – think how much you teach your children daily. To top it off, once you see how flexible and lucrative it can be (see Chapter 4), even on a part-time basis, it may become even more attractive to you.

Training is important in the computer-age we live in. Companies train their employees so they can take advantage of high-tech tools to improve overall efficiency, productivity, data integrity, and quality control. As an instructor, you are performing an important service by educating people and giving them new skills for better performance, record-keeping, and decision-making.

From Microsoft to other popular software programs, there are many opportunities available. This chapter highlights what it takes to be an instructor, as well as a few of the more popular training and software choices.

THE RIGHT STUFF

One day I was talking to a friend of mine who was disappointed because his employer did not give him a good performance evaluation. A technical person, he was responsible for managing a group of non-technical people. After his review, he was considering quitting his job to go out on his own and become an instructor.

When I asked what had gone wrong in the review, he said his boss felt that he was condescending to and impatient with the employees that he supervised. When I heard that, I laughed, and said, "Well, you can't be an instructor and be that way with your students!"

WHY WOULD THIS WORK FOR YOU?

Becoming an instructor takes a special kind of personality, one that requires a lot of energy and patience. For an in-depth discussion on patience and professional behavior, see Chapters 1 and 14, respectively. Most women who have kids are patient (and/or have a lot of energy!), simply because they have to be!

Women are smart, strong, creative, capable, and resourceful. In today's high-tech world, an increasing number of women are computer literate. Some hold degrees or have studied computers, information technology, computer networking, programming, or systems administration. In general, more women hold college degrees today than at any previous time in human history.

Training works for people who prefer short-term projects. A class lasts two or three days, and then it's over. You have to have enough high energy to last through the class, and then you can recuperate afterwards. There is no long drawn out consulting project, during which you'd be sitting behind a desk for weeks on end.

Personally, training keeps me challenged because I teach a different software class every week. I know that I have to keep my knowledge current and my skills sharp in order to teach the class. Most instructors also enjoy meeting and getting to know the diverse group of students whom they teach.

Training is the perfect job for moms, because it allows for a flexible schedule working a few days per month. Two women I know (both new moms who copied my business model) obtained contracts at large corporations teaching one week each month. Both make more than enough money to pay their bills, but still have ample time to stay home with their daughters. If this sounds like the right fit for you, then you may want to consider becoming an instructor.

TEACHING CERTIFICATIONS

Many software manufacturers offer Certified (or Authorized) Training Programs to independent instructors (non-employees). By design, teaching certifications, like the technical certifications discussed in Chapter 6, are not necessarily easy to obtain. Many have stringent requirements, including a certain number of years of work, project, or public speaking experience, a difficult exam, and demonstrated proficiency in a software or technology via presentation or a "hands-on" test. In addition, many are tiered, meaning that you must obtain a lower level certification first, before you can apply for a higher-level certification.

Certified training programs have several advantages. For example, these programs benefit the manufacturers because they typically charge a healthy fee for instructors to use their name. The fee for teaching certifications may be one of your most expensive start-up costs. These fees can range anywhere from a few hundred dollars to a few thousand dollars annually per certification, depending on what field you're in.

From a marketing standpoint, certifications provide a way for manufacturers to increase their visibility by reaching more customers (yours). The benefit to you is that all course materials (slides, books and course certificates) are provided by the manufacturer, which saves you a lot of time you would have otherwise spent developing your own materials.

Another advantage is that certifications provide increased credibility, especially if you are not initially well-known in your field. Many manufacturers list their certified instructors on their websites for advertising purposes, so that potential customers can contact you directly. This alone is often worth the certification fee, especially if it is a major website that receives a lot of traffic or hits from the company's customers. By all means, take advantage of this "website marketing," but don't count on it as a sole source of leads. You will still have to actively sell yourself (see Chapter 4).

What follows is a list of some of the more common teaching certifications available from some of the more recognizable software companies. The information presented in this chapter is not intended to be a comprehensive list. Other companies may offer certification programs that are not as well-known or widely advertised, including Microsoft Visio (diagramming and flowcharting software), 3D StudioMAX (3D visualization and animation software), and Pervasive® software. You may also find additional certifications or software in your specific industry or field of expertise that are not listed here. (Note: Listing does not imply endorsement.)

MICROSOFT TEACHING CERTIFICATIONS

As mentioned in Chapter 6, Microsoft Corporation is one of the most recognized names in the computer industry. Microsoft develops and manufactures all types of software and operating systems, from the popular MS Office Suite (which, depending on the edition, includes Word, Excel, Outlook, Publisher, Powerpoint, and the Access database programs) to the various Microsoft Windows operating systems. Microsoft offers several training certifications for its products. For more information, please go to www.microsoft.com. (Note: All links listed are subject to change.)

- MCT, or Microsoft Certified Trainer. MCTs are qualified instructors, regarded as Microsoft product and course experts certified by Microsoft to deliver training courses to IT professionals and developers. Certification as an MCT demonstrates proficiency in various Microsoft software products, and can also complement any of the technical certifications found in Chapter 6 (meaning that you are not only certified to actually *do* the work, but that you can also teach classes in that specific certification).
- Microsoft Office Specialist Master Instructor. The Microsoft Office Specialist Master Instructors are certified trainers of Microsoft Office desktop programs. These software products include Word, Excel, PowerPoint, Outlook, Publisher, and the Access database program, as well as the various Windows operating systems.

ADOBE® CERTIFICATIONS

Founded in 1982 and headquartered in San Jose, California, Adobe Systems, Inc., is one of the largest software companies in the world. Adobe specializes in digital imaging software and graphics programs, including Adobe Photoshop®, PageMaker, and FrameMaker®. Adobe also manufacturers Acrobat® Reader®, the free download program that reads those ubiquitous PDF (Portable Document Format) files.

Adobe offers certification as an Adobe Certified Expert (ACE), or "power-user," and as an Adobe Certified Instructor (ACI). In order to become an ACI, you must first be an ACE. Adobe Certified Instructors are authorized to provide instruction on Adobe software products. (For more information, please go to www.adobe.com.)

MACROMEDIA®

MacroMedia, headquartered in San Francisco, California, develops and manufactures many popular Web development software programs, including Dreamweaver®, and Macromedia Flash MX Designer and Developer. Macromedia has an Authorized Training Program (MATP) open to select partners. MacroMedia Certified Professionals (MCP) are recognized across the industry as experts in Web design, application development, programming, and database design. (For more information please go to www.macromedia.com.)

NOVELL

As mentioned previously in Chapter 6, Novell was one of the first companies to offer commercial networking software and information technology (IT) solutions. Today, in addition to networking services, Novell offers Linux support, Web services and application integration, and cross-platform computer networking.

Novell offers certifications in several key areas, including consulting, sales, technical support, and educational services. (For a list of Novell non-teaching certifications, see Chapter 6). Currently, Novell offers certification as a Certified Novell Instructor (CNI). (Please go to www.novell.com for more information and specific certification requirements.)

AUTOCAD®

Manufactured by Autodesk®, AutoCAD (Computer-Aided-Design) is the market-leading drafting software. AutoCAD is used by engineers, architects, and the construction industry to design and model buildings, stadiums, bridges, and other infrastructure. Autodesk operates many AutoCAD Authorized Training Centers worldwide. ATC instructors must be certified. (Contact Autodesk directly at www.autodesk.com for more information.)

WHAT IF NO CERTIFICATION PROGRAM IS AVAILABLE?

Not all software companies offer certified training programs. In other words, software classes are only taught in-house by employees. An example is Crystal Reports®, the market-leading desktop query and report writer. Crystal Reports is used to report or query directly from data sources, provide reports, or produce a report inside of other database applications. Users can perform powerful data analysis with presentation-quality output. Crystal Reports is a stand-alone reporting program, but it can also be found embedded in many other software products. Select third-party training is available through www.crystaluser.com.

Other software ripe for teaching includes QuickBooks® (accounting and bookkeeping software), ACT!™ database software, Adobe FrameMaker, Microsoft FrontPage, and Primavera® or other project management software. Specialty image processing software such as ENVI, ERDAS, PCI, or Idrisi. Airline reservations software. Accountants use Peachtree® and Quicken. What about programming languages? C'mon! There must be something.

Think about what you do for a living. Do you use a certain type or brand of software in your daily work? Is it possible for you to teach this software out on your own? What about people at other companies or vendors who use the same software that you do? Could you start out by offering classes to them?

Because certified training programs provide books and slides to authorized instructors, if none exists for the software you are familiar with, then you may be faced with creating your own courses and course materials. Writing your own course materials can be time consuming (up to 3 weeks for a 2-day course!), not to mention expensive because you have to pay for the copy and binding. However, creating your own materials does give you more control over the class content. (For more on the pros and cons of developing your own course materials, see the interview with Leita Hart, CPA, in Chapter 5.)

FRANCHISE COURSES

As discussed in Chapter 6, another option you may want to consider is purchasing a franchise. Many "ready-made" training courses are available from franchises, including courses in leadership development, communication and negotiation skills, interpersonal techniques, organizational dynamics, conflict resolution and managing emotions, productivity improvement, and time management skills. Although purchasing a franchise can cost up to several thousand dollars, there are many advantages to doing so.

Celia Thompkins, a CPA who was laid off from a high-tech manufacturing company, used her severance pay to purchase a franchise business specializing in leadership development. Celia says, "I was browsing the Internet and I found Leadership Management, Inc. I sent them a resume and looked at their materials. I decided it was a good fit, so I paid the franchise fee. It was a lot of money, but I didn't have to develop my own materials."

She continues, "I moved from accounting to the consulting side. The franchise allowed me to leverage their 30 plus years of experience in the leadership development area, but I went out and developed my own clients. It allowed me to get started right away, instead of spending time developing my own materials. Ninety days later I had my first client."

OTHER TEACHING OPTIONS

If software is not your thing, how about some kind of part-time teaching in your field? Is there a complicated topic in your field of expertise? Could you develop your own course or one-day seminar for that topic? There is always a demand for experienced, knowledgeable instructors who can provide direction and guidance to newcomers.

For instance, I know a woman who teaches classes at the local community college on how to start up your own medical billing business using industry specific billing software. She pioneered the medical billing practice in the early 1990s when doctors first began to outsource complicated insurance billing, and she has been doing it for more than ten years. Her many years of real work experience and resulting wisdom benefit her students.

OTHER THOUGHTS

If you decide to teach classes, don't rent a training facility at first, which can be an expensive option. Instead, start out by offering on-site training at the client's office. These classes are not only easier to fill, but there is also less risk of a class getting cancelled than if you have scheduled an "open" class (a.k.a. public seminars or workshops) and are trying to fill it yourself.

MIX IT UP

If you can't decide whether you want to be a consultant, an instructor, or a writer, why not combine all of them? That's what I do. When I first started out on my own, back in 1996, I didn't start out necessarily wanting to be an instructor, but I knew it was a marketable skill because I had teaching certifications from both a GPS and GIS company. I also knew enough about both fields to provide specialized expertise in the form of consulting and technical writing.

Today, I have built up each area of my business enough so that I am as busy as I want to be. Keep an open mind and don't pigeonhole yourself. You may discover a hidden strength, skill, or something you otherwise enjoy that can ultimately be used to expand the list of services you offer.

PRESENTATION SKILLS AND TRAINING TECHNIQUES

If you are going to teach classes, you must be able to stand up in front of a group and give a talk. Even if you don't want to teach, there comes a time in everyone's career when you will have to give some kind of a public presentation. It's inevitable. Plus, if you want to be successful, be a leader, or well-respected in your field, then at some point you will need to be able to speak in front of a group. It's that simple.

Many knowledgeable books have been written on public speaking, therefore I will only try to summarize a few tips that I have found useful during my career. Chapter 14, "Being a Professional," features some additional communication skills for dealing with difficult students or classroom situations, as well as techniques for dealing with burnout.

The most important thing you can do when speaking in front of a group is to be knowledgeable, prepared, and confident. Know your topic. Keep in mind that you are the Subject Matter Expert (SME); in other words, you know a lot more about whatever subject you are speaking about than your audience does.

Establish your credibility by stating your experience when you introduce yourself. For example, say "My name is _____, and I have been working in this field for more than five years." When speaking, keep your hands away from your face, mouth, and hair. Nervous gestures such as pushing your hair behind your ear are distracting and detract from your overall professionalism.

Keep a tight schedule, and be on time. When teaching or giving a seminar, if you have trouble with participants coming back late from a break, try writing the time to return on the board. You can also project the computer clock onto the large screen.

When writing something down in front of a group, don't speak at the same time you are facing the whiteboard. The whiteboard may be able to hear you, but the audience won't! Always face your audience when speaking to them. After you finish a topic and want to move on to the next, erase what you have written on the board. This simple action provides a "clean slate" and a good transition for introducing the next topic.

It's easy for attendees to become overwhelmed and over-saturated with too much material, especially when classes are more than one day long. Keep your slides uncluttered by limiting your bullet points to only two or three per slide.

Don't read your slides! Your students can do that. Use your slides as talking points and elaborate on each bullet or concept by drawing upon your own experience and knowledge.

If you notice your audience becoming glassy-eyed, you can introduce a fun brainteaser type activity. I keep a packet of these handouts in my briefcase, and I use them to break up long monotonous lessons. I hope that you will find these suggestions helpful, so that _you_ don't become too overwhelmed and over-saturated when giving a presentation!

CHAPTER 12

Jennifer Harrison
Independent Instructor

Jennifer "Jenny" Harrison is an independent instructor who lives in Houston, Texas. In 1999, the consulting company she worked for closed down its training department, and Jenny made the decision to go it alone and work part time. With a Bachelor's degree in Math, and a Master's in GeoSciences, Jenny was more than qualified to go out on her own.

Today she teaches custom scripting (programming) languages and high-end software programs to a host of oil and gas clients in the Houston area. Married with three children, Jenny quickly realized that working for herself provided her with more freedom, flexibility, and time to spend with her large family.

Jenny moved to Houston in 1994, after her husband decided to pursue a Ph.D. at Rice University. Previously, they had been living in Belize, where her husband taught at the University of Belize, and Jenny worked in natural resources management for the government. Six months after arriving in Houston, Jenny was recruited by a consulting company, who liked the fact that she had international work experience.

While employed by the consulting company, Jenny worked on contract for five years teaching classes and consulting for a major oil and gas firm. When her employer was bought out, the new owners offered Jenny a full-time consulting job, which she turned down in favor of continuing to teach classes out on her own.

She says, "When the new company closed down the training department, the materials and the client were still in place, so I took over the courses on my own. Both the consulting company and the client were happy with this situation. I didn't have much overhead, and thankfully, I didn't have to do much course development. I did have to revise some old books and update the material. I went out and filed a DBA (Doing Business As) to get started, and set up a home office."

She continues, "At the time, my husband was also independent, so we were paying through the nose for health insurance. Just as our COBRA benefits were about to run out, my husband was offered a full-time position, and I was able to get on his health insurance, which gave us more flexibility. There was a three month lag before I taught my first class after going out on my own. We cut our expenses and I spent those three months staying home with my kids."

Many people who are successful at establishing their own businesses have had parents who worked for themselves as role models. In Jenny's case, she credits her parents for helping her make the decision to go out on her own. "One thing that helped me go out on my own was the fact that my Mom and Dad started several different businesses when I was a kid, and I had an idea how much work it is to run your own business. My Mom had a small restaurant, where she was the cook, waitress, manager and accountant. My brothers and I helped in every aspect of that business (doing paper work, going to the grocery, waiting tables, cooking, etc.), and that business supported us through high school. My Mom worked hard, but she was her own boss."

Jenny talks about the freedom she now has versus when she was working full time for the consulting firm. "When I worked full time, I was working 12 hour days. Plus, the client was 45 minutes away from my house, and I didn't like the commute or the traffic. At the time, my oldest daughter was in the third grade."

"Looking back, I don't know how I did it. I had absolutely no flexibility in my schedule. I couldn't leave my job to go to lunch at her school or help out the school party. When my daughter's school was closed, I had to use my vacation time to stay home with her. Now I can not only help out at my children's schools when needed, but I also see my kids a lot more. My oldest daughter will be 18 soon, my other daughter is eight, and my son is six. I have a lot of flexibility in my schedule on days that I am not teaching. For instance, I pick them up from school when they are done at 2:30 P.M., and I am a Girl Scout Leader for my youngest daughter. I realize now I would've missed a lot if I were still working a full-time job."

Since starting out in 1999, Jenny has continually added classes and clients to her repertoire. Her main client is still the oil and gas firm, which schedules its classes out at least one year in advance. Jenny teaches PERL, UNIX, several programming languages, GIS, and other specialized software used by the petroleum industry. She frequently customizes her classes to meet the specific needs of her clients. Many of her current clients knew her when she was still at the consulting firm. Eventually the word spread and Jenny was able to build up her business through client referrals.

Maintaining her professional reputation is very important to Jenny. "I built up my credibility by offering a free slot in my classes to some of my clients. This allows a potential client to get to know me. Sometimes I go to a client's office and spend an hour or two helping them with a simple task on the computer. Then they will hire me later to teach a class."

Jenny talks about the commitment required to be an instructor. "When you're an instructor, you must be professional, which means you can't cancel a class. There is no flexibility on days you are teaching. When you have a class scheduled you must be there, even if it means missing your child's school play, which happened to me once. I have only missed a few classes, once when I had meningitis, and once when my grandmother died. These were real emergencies. If you're going to be an instructor out on your own, you must take it seriously. It's important to understand that while your students can miss a class for any reason, you certainly can't."

Although living in a large metropolitan area (Houston is the fourth largest city in the United States) is definitely a benefit to an independent consultant, sometimes travel is still a necessity. Last year Jenny secured a contract teaching one week per month in Louisiana. She says being gone was very hard on her kids, and she even noticed a change in her children's personalities.

Fortunately, Jenny's husband, while working a very demanding full-time job himself, also has some flexibility to work from home, and picks up the slack while she is gone. Jenny's oldest daughter is also a tremendous help, picking up her younger brother and sister and driving them to their numerous activities when Jenny is out of town. Even with her family's help, Jenny recently opened up a training center in Houston so she doesn't have to travel anymore.

She elaborates, "Traveling can be very stressful on your relationships if you're gone a lot. I decided to try and limit my travel by opening up a training center so my students could come to me. I rented an office and purchased ten computers. Starting out, I taught on-site classes only. To my surprise, I found that the training center gave me additional credibility. I had an address and an office for my clients to visit. I also found that many of my in-town clients would rather come to me than travel out-of-town to a regional training center to take a class."

Jenny has gained a lot of invaluable insight, experience, and wisdom since going out on her own. Fortunately, she is willing to share her knowledge with others. "If you are going to go out on your own, don't expect to make a lot of money in the beginning. You are going to have to work extremely hard. You may have to start out at $20 per hour, rather than $100 per hour. Don't go out and eat steak every night, eat a grilled cheese sandwich. Once you have built up your experience and reputation, then you can charge more. Also, don't think you can do this job after you put your kids to bed. You will be too tired. Spend that time with your husband. If you are an instructor who teaches full time, be sure to take on occasional consulting work. This will give you real-world experience for the classroom as well as keep your skills fresh; both of which are very important to a trainer."

For Jenny Harrison, working part time as an instructor gives her the flexibility she needs to spend time with her family. She says, "The reason that I like working as a trainer is that I get to see the sunshine. At the consulting firm I was billing every hour, and I couldn't take the time to go to conferences. Now I can attend industry conferences and network while I am there. I have the flexibility to schedule my classes around my family."

Last year Jenny was able to take three weeks off around Christmas to be with her kids. She describes the flexibility that comes with having your own business this way, "Some people who have worked for 20 years with one company only get four weeks of vacation per year. Even though when a class is scheduled I HAVE to be there, I can leave my week open and not schedule a class during holidays when my kids are off. In summary, don't work part time if you think it's going to be easy or that you're going to get rich. It's the flexibility you are gaining that's important." ·

I couldn't have said it better myself.

Many thanks to Jenny Harrison, my friend and colleague, who can be reached at:

Inner Corridor Technologies
3000 Wilcrest, Suite 195
Houston, Texas 77042

CHAPTER 13

Public Speaking

A re you a former career woman turned stay-at-home mom? Did you have a great career when you were working? Why not put that knowledge and experience to work helping a room full of people?

WHO ARE PUBLIC SPEAKERS?

Professional speakers hail from a variety of industries and disciplines, including instructors, trainers and educators, coaches, humorists, motivators, consultants, and writers/authors (notice that nearly all of the professions featured in this book are on the list). One of the good things about making a living as a public speaker is that it's possible to make a lot of money in a short amount of time. This situation may be ideal for former career women in their 30s or 40s (or older), who are looking for a flexible way to re-enter the workforce or switch careers.

Some speakers are Subject Matter Experts (SMEs), or otherwise have a specialty, niche, or certain area of expertise. If you start out as an instructor (see Chapter 11), you have an advantage because you can hone your speaking skills and gain confidence while teaching classes.

Is there a complex area in your field that you could simplify and talk about to others? A Certified Public Accountant (CPA) can focus on financial and accounting topics (see Chapter 5, Leita Hart). Two lawyers I know conduct seminars in elder law and employment law, both specialty areas of the legal profession. Speaking for myself, I have given plenty of talks on GPS (Global Positioning System) and GIS (Geographic

Information Systems), and how the combined technologies are used to-gether.

Public speakers must be credible. Perhaps after you have established yourself first as an independent consultant, instructor, or author, you will have enough credibility to try your hand as a public speaker. How do you build credibility if you don't have it? Read Chapter 4, "Selling Yourself," for specific proven ideas to establish credibility.

WHAT WOULD I SAY?

The main thing is to keep it interesting. In today's society, public speakers are essentially entertainers. If you can be entertaining by holding the audience's attention during the entire presentation, then you have done a good job.

Talk about what you know. If you are a recognized expert in any field, or have a specific niche or area of expertise (including parenting), then you have valuable knowledge and experience to share with others. Speakers who specialize in interesting subjects are always in demand. (I am fortunate because GPS is a fascinating topic with widespread appeal.)

Give your audience something of value. If your audience comes away with some new information they did not have before they heard you speak, they will consider their time with you worthwhile. It can be a new idea, new technique (e.g., communication skill, or technical "know-how" they can apply in their job), personal "war story," humorous anecdote, parenting story/solution, or something else.

It helps if you read a great deal on a lot of different topics. You never know when a previously useless piece of trivia can come in handy during a relevant point in a presentation. When a football player takes a ballet class, it is called training "outside their area." The idea is that a technique learned in the ballet class might come in handy during a football game to enhance the player's performance. The same is true of information.

Don't read your slides! The audience can do that. Use your slides as talking points and elaborate on each bullet or concept by drawing upon your own experience and knowledge.

Another tip is know when to quit. Respect other people's time. Don't keep on talking just because you are nervous and/or have a captive audience.

I once attended a college career fair, and the first speaker took up much more than his allotted time. He went on and on about how great his company was to work for, and then pontificated to the point that the poor students were bored and glassy-eyed. Nobody cut him off or asked him to stop, and unfortunately after he was finally done none of the students wanted to listen to anybody else!

Make your point and then stop. Rehearse aloud what you are going to say beforehand. Don't go off on long tangents or ramble on. One of the hallmarks of a great public speaker is being able to read the audience and know when to quit (or switch gears by taking a break, changing the subject, making a joke, etc.).

To speak in public, you do not have to be perfect. You do not have to give your audience every single detail on the topic you are speaking about. For a short presentation, it is better to talk in broad terms anyway.

One well-kept secret about public speaking is that most people in the audience don't know or notice what you leave out or don't say. I first realized this from watching two different weathermen on our local news. Because Austin is such a haven for pollen producing trees and plants, allergies are very common. One weatherman gives an in-depth allergy forecast, while the other skips over it as fast as he can because it's not his forté. Because the latter is so well-respected, nobody even notices. For more on presentation skills, tips, and techniques, see Chapter 11.

SIX POINTERS TO REMEMBER WHEN GIVING A PRESENTATION

1. Keep it interesting.
2. Talk about what you know.
3. Give your audience something of value (some new information they learn and/or leave with). Make them feel like they benefited from listening to you.
4. Don't read the slides.
5. Know when to quit. (Don't ramble on.)
6. Nobody will know or notice what you omit.

WHO DO I TALK TO?

There is always a need for experienced, knowledgeable, professional speakers who can give workshops, training, lectures, talks, and keynote addresses for various meetings. What type of meetings? Industry, technical, and women's conferences, trade shows, seminars, and professional groups and organizations.

Conferences and trade shows need keynote speakers, and people to lead breakout sessions and workshops. (Keynotes pay more than the latter, but are harder to land, unless you are famous or a very experienced speaker.) Talks can be given to peer groups (e.g., book clubs), and groups that meet for breakfast or lunch (e.g., professional organizations, or Rotary or Kiwanis Clubs). Local libraries and churches often host free talks or lectures.

Research professional organizations in your field and others. There are plenty to choose from – computer security professionals (ISC^2), CPAs, bankers, engineers (e.g., IEEE and others), and surveyors, to name a few. Most of these professional associations have annual, quarterly, or monthly meetings.

Surveyors and engineers who are in business for themselves may want to hear a CPA talk about accounting topics (tips on how to keep their books). The Society of CPAs may want someone to come in and talk about communication skills, so that their members can improve their client relationships, and thus gain more business. Lawyers can speak about specific areas of the law to other attorneys, corporations, non-profit groups, and other organizations. The list goes on and on.

Like anything else, building a career in public speaking takes time and dedication. Many prospective speakers start out speaking on a pro-bono basis in their topic of expertise. Volunteering as a moderator at a trade show or conference provides a means to making valuable contacts and getting to know the conference coordinators (who might hire you next year as a speaker). Eventually you will become established and build up your client base. At that time, you can begin to request small honorariums for your presentations, which will lead to paid speaking engagements.

SPEAKERS BUREAUS

A speakers bureau is a for profit organization that locates speakers for paying clients. Many meeting planners and conference coordinators use speakers bureaus to find and book professional speakers. Normally, the bureau takes a percentage of your gross fee for every booking they make for you.

Speakers bureaus typically exist in each major city and supply appropriate speakers to fit an event. You must furnish the bureau with promotional materials that don't contain your contact information, so that potential clients will contact the bureau directly and not you. Requirements to be registered with a speakers bureau vary, so check with your local office.

NATIONAL SPEAKERS ASSOCIATION

As opposed to a speakers bureau, the National Speakers Association (NSA) is a leading organization for those who make their living from professional speaking. Speakers benefit both from the programs offered by NSA, and from the prestige of being an NSA member. Most of the programs hosted through NSA are designed to help you build your speaking business and/or become a better speaker. NSA has local chapters, by city, that typically meet once per month.

NSA membership gives you credibility. One of the requirements is to have a certain number of speaking engagements under your belt, therefore a potential client already knows you have a proven track record before they hire you. NSA membership can be listed on your resume or business card for marketing purposes.

If you don't qualify for NSA membership initially, some chapters let you attend as a guest until you do. NSA also offers a training academy to help newcomers make the leap into professional public speaking. Many of the local chapters have an apprentice program designed to help you obtain speaking engagements so you can join NSA. Check with your local chapter for specifics and additional information.

CSP

We learned in previous chapters that certifications increase your credibility. A CSP is a Certified Speaking Professional designation awarded through the NSA. The letters CSP following a speaker's name indicate a speaking professional with proven experience and skill who knows how to deliver client satisfaction.

The requirements for obtaining a CSP are strict. You must have a lot of experience and a certain number of booked speaking engagements. NSA offers programs to help speakers obtain a CSP designation.

If you are scared to death to even think about speaking in public, I don't blame you. Almost everyone is at first. Like anything else, practice makes it easier. Join Toastmasters first (as the name implies, an organization dedicated to helping people master public speaking skills), and who knows – you may become a pro and ultimately decide to pursue a CSP certification. Regardless of what you decide, public speaking can be a flexible, satisfying career, as well as a means to personal growth through conquering fear and trying something new. If you try it, you might be surprised to find that you like it.

CHAPTER 14

Being a Professional

What exactly does *professional* mean anyway? Generally the term refers to a specific type of profession (doctors and lawyers, for example), or working people who hold college degrees. However, *being professional* also refers to a type of behavior, or a "code of conduct." It is the manner in which you carry yourself, regardless of your field.

Professional behavior is a deliberate method of thinking, and it may require a shift in your modus operandi. As stated previously, your business must be a priority and not treated as a hobby. As a business owner and consultant, one of your top goals should be to keep your customers happy. This chapter offers tips on providing customer service and handling situations in a professional manner.

PROFESSIONAL BEHAVIOR

In Chapter 1, we discussed the "Top Ten Qualities Required to Start a Business," including maturity, self-discipline, and communication skills. These same qualities are an essential part of professional conduct. This means when you are irritated with students because they don't know how to perform a simple task on their computer, such as how to save a file, you can't yell at them or call them boneheads (even though you might be thinking it!).

You must possess the self-discipline, patience, and grace to smile and bite your tongue. Moreover, your students must not be able to sense your irritation. Being a professional means being able to own up to something, admit when you're wrong, and apologize if necessary.

Once my husband and I went to eat dinner at a fancy restaurant. We waited a long time for a table, and by the time we were finally seated it was close to closing time. As the hostess was seating us, the young waiter gave her a dirty look, presumably because he wanted to go home, rather than serve us. Obviously, by showing his displeasure, our waiter didn't act professionally and therefore didn't keep his customers happy, all of which did little to enhance our dining experience (or his tip!).

RETURN PHONE CALLS

Make an effort to return all phone calls and e-mails promptly. If you are in the office, answer the phone in person rather than let the call go to voice mail. I have received jobs several times simply because I answered the phone and the client was thrilled to actually speak to a live person rather than a recording.

When you are teaching a class or are out of the office, calls are still coming in, so check your messages regularly, and return all calls promptly. You cannot make a go of your business without returning phone calls or answering e-mails. If you work out of the house, try to eliminate background noise when you are on a business call. Set aside some dedicated time each day when you can talk on the phone without distractions.

Answer the phone with a smile on your face. People can hear it in your voice. I once had a client tell me he always enjoyed calling me because I was always so happy to hear from him. Don't you think that kept him coming back?

COMMUNICATION SKILLS

Being professional means learning and applying some simple communication skills when dealing with clients and colleagues. This requires you to be logical, not emotional, and to think before you speak, a task that doesn't always come easy. By learning some simple communication techniques, you can keep from burning bridges. This is important because your reputation, networking, and referrals all depend on it.

First, learn to practice discretion. This means not telling everybody everything you know. Don't share confidences and secrets (yours or other people's) with anyone else. Keep them just that – secret!

Sometimes it behooves you to withhold extraneous information. Don't criticize other people, and keep your problems and sad stories to yourself.

Nothing turns people off faster than unloading your personal problems on them, and they don't belong in a professional atmosphere anyway.

A colleague of mine does not have a college degree. Now, this is not a big deal. In fact, most people who meet him would never even know or care, because he is an intelligent and likeable person. However, it obviously bothers him, because he inevitably mentions this fact in passing conversation to almost everybody he meets. The point is that if he didn't say anything, nobody would ever know. Why tell people what they don't need to know?

Second, learn to validate what other people say. This is a tough one, because for some reason, most people instinctively and immediately contradict what others say and think that they, themselves, are right. Tact is the ability to make your point without making an enemy.

If you disagree with someone, need to resolve a conflict, or are dealing with a difficult client or situation, use a technique called "framing" or "frontloading" the message. Say something like "I can certainly understand your perspective; however, you may not have considered . . . ." Then state your position. There are many "validation phrases" you can use, and they all work amazingly well to dissipate a potential confrontation *and* keep differing opinions in check.

IMAGE

Another aspect of being professional involves your image. In Chapter 4 we learned that looking good helps to boost your credibility. For women, looking good means dressing conservatively.

If you want to make a positive impression, wear a professional business suit. When you buy a new outfit, don't skimp on the shoes. Spend the money for nice shoes, and while you're at it, get a very good, flattering haircut, and regular trims. Every so often, get a makeover and update your look.

CUSTOMER SERVICE

The other day I saw a sign that said, "Customer service is an attitude, not a department." That is so true!

Have you ever been to a doctor who was brusque and/or impatient with his patients? Did the experience make you want to go back? Probably

111

not. I have always maintained that you can go to school and learn how to be a doctor, lawyer, veterinarian or whatever, but that doesn't mean you know how to treat people with professionalism and courtesy. Customer service and communication skills go hand in hand.

In addition to receiving good value for their money (see the discussion on rates in Chapter 4), your clients want to be treated with respect, concern, caring, and promptness.

Notice and acknowledge your clients and make them feel important. Congratulate them when they receive good news. Their good news is your good news, and may translate into more business for you.

Be conscientious and considerate. If you say you're going to do something, then follow through and do it. And it goes without saying not to make any promises you can't keep!

One company I used to work with (we'll call it ABC Company) was in the business of repairing technical equipment. One of its clients sent in a piece of equipment for repair, and the repairs turned out to be much more extensive than originally anticipated. Instead of calling the client first and asking if he wanted to spend the extra money on the additional repairs, ABC went ahead and did the work anyway, then sent a huge bill for the additional time and materials.

The client was furious! If he had known ahead of time about the additional expense, the client could have shopped around for several estimates, or even decided to buy a brand new piece of equipment, which ultimately would have cost less than the repair job. Lesson learned? Never assume. When in doubt, call your client first and ask. Then *listen* to what he or she has to say.

To ensure good service, always get your work done on time. Never miss a deadline, and give the client more than he expects. For example, when I teach, I often offer to install the software on the computers the day before the class. I try to take care of as many details as I can from my end, which saves the client the time and hassle of doing it himself.

The bottom line is that if you are good at what you do, are likeable and easy to work with, and can provide good customer service, then the word will spread about your business. It's as simple as that.

Look at the cruise lines. They are an example of a successful industry because they figure out what people want and provide it. People like to be pampered, and cruise lines specialize in providing exceptional service. Why do you think cruise vacations are so popular, and so many people take cruises over and over again?

KEEP YOURSELF UP TO DATE

In addition to updating your image periodically, you also need to keep your technical skills up to date. When you are self-employed, that is not always an easy thing to do. However, as fast as technology changes today (new computers are obsolete in only a few months), it is imperative that you make an effort to keep current in your field.

One idea is to attend industry conference and trade shows in your field. Cynthia Long, a computer project manager profiled in Chapter 3, attends at least two technical conferences a year in her field, InterOp and NetWorld. She also attends national and local meetings of the Project Management Institute. Another method that works well is to subscribe to and read industry magazines.

Keeping technical skills up to date when you are self-employed is harder for some women than for others. Ann Kasunich, a marketing professional profiled in Chapter 10, says "That is really hard, but you must do it. I read a lot, and I intermittently attend the American Marketing Association (AMA) monthly meetings. It comes down to trade-offs in your schedule. Going to the meetings can be really helpful and you might miss an opportunity if you don't show up. Ultimately I need to go each month, but my schedule doesn't always work out that way."

Sometimes, simply interacting and meeting other people in your industry can generate positive energy, creativity, and new ideas. Leita Hart, a CPA profiled in Chapter 5, expands on this concept: "I have to attend a lot of training seminars myself. I also read industry magazines. Other CPAs I meet at those meetings go back to their organization and then I end up training for them. Ultimately, all these interactions feed off each other."

DEALING WITH BURNOUT AND BOREDOM

Let's face it – teaching (or anything else) can be a high burnout profession. In fact, most instructor positions are considered "ground-floor" or entry-level positions at large corporations. The reason? High turnover.

Burnout can happen no matter what field you are in. I have been going strong as an instructor for ten years and have some tips to keep boredom and burnout from setting in.

Have a positive attitude. I know it sounds cliché, but it's amazing how much your attitude controls your life. Refresh your skills and keep them up to date.

Teach a variety of classes. Challenge yourself occasionally by teaching a new class or a class outside your comfort zone. If you're not stimulated with your work, take up a mentally challenging extracurricular activity or new hobby. Some ideas include sailing, tennis, karate, golf, chess, bridge, book clubs, woodworking, or learning a foreign language.

The bottom line is to keep a positive attitude and don't let yourself become bored or burned out. That is part of being professional – doing something even if you don't feel like it.

TOP TEN QUALITIES REQUIRED FOR BEING PROFESSIONAL

1. Patience and self-discipline.
2. Return phone calls and e-mails promptly.
3. Practice discretion by not telling everyone everything you know!
4. Learn good communication skills.
5. Keep yourself up-to-date and have pride in your personal appearance.
6. Be conscientious and considerate by noticing things about other people, especially your customers.
7. Never miss a deadline.
8. Keep your technical skills up to date and challenge yourself periodically.
9. Have a positive attitude.
10. Don't let other people sense your moods. Do things with a smile on your face, even if you don't feel like it!

CHAPTER 15

Beni Patel
Consultant

In 1994, the year I met her, Beni Patel was working full time as a research analyst for a non-profit facility. Two years later, at the age of 31, Beni became pregnant with her first child, Niki. At the time, Beni decided to reprioritize her life so that her family came first. She knew she wanted to expand her family and have a second child, and she wanted to be out on her own before that happened.

Beni is now the mother of two daughters, Niki, now eight, and Maya, five. She has attained all of her goals. Not only is she is a successful independent consultant with many clients, but more importantly, she has the flexibility she needs in her life to put her family first.

In 1996, Beni left her stable full-time job to pursue being her own boss. At first, she and a friend partnered up to form their own cyber-company. An idea ahead of its time (at the time), the two women telecommuted and did work remotely, meaning not at the client site. They eventually sold their idea to a larger company, who infused their operation with start-up capital. The arrangement worked well for awhile, until Beni's partner accepted a job with another company.

According to Beni, "When my partner left, I wasn't ready to go with her. Then, the person who was the champion for us and our idea also quit, and all of a sudden I found myself on the outside. I ended up negotiating a deal with the company to buy all of their hardware, equipment, and software. Now I was on my own using the business model we had originally sold to that company. I wasn't scared, I was just ready to do it."

She continues, "I decided I wanted to have an organization that valued family life, and I needed to control my time. I built up a network of people who could work together when needed. My thinking was that if I had many high energy people who could work independently, then why did we need to work in a common place, or even for the same company? That is the business model that I basically use today."

Beni's work experience combined with two Master's Degrees, one in Forestry, and one in Environmental Science, gave her a unique set of skills. Eight years after going out on her own, Beni has built up an impressive clientele. For private sector clients, she provides on-site consulting, which requires her physical presence at the client's office, where she performs high-level needs assessment and database design. She has also done remote sensing, data modeling, computer application development, and research projects for universities. Her projects (and thus her contracts) usually last six months to a year at a time.

In addition to consulting, Beni fills in as a software instructor when needed. She holds several teaching certifications from well-known software companies, although she prefers not to market herself specifically as a trainer. She says, "The certifications give me additional credibility, and training will often lead to other work. I teach maybe two or three classes per year, definitely not full time." Beni also teaches at a local university once a year, which keeps her on her toes and forces her to keep abreast of technology.

Expanding on the topic of credibility, Beni says, "I built up my business through word of mouth. In fact, I didn't even have a business card the first four years I was on my own. I knew a lot of people through my previous job. One thing I did do right off the bat to increase my credibility was to incorporate. I have found that being a corporation [versus a sole proprietor] can make it easier to work with large companies."

Above all, Beni values the freedom, flexibility, and quality time with her family that her status as an independent consultant provides. "The best part is control of my time. Spending time with my family is so important because we are losing family life in America. Family life is no longer valued, and we are losing out as a society. I am able to take off for every school holiday and be there with my kids. I mark their vacations on my calendar and don't work those days. My husband recently started working from home, so one of us is there when our kids come home. Many people must work two jobs and can't look after their children, so I am very thankful to be out on my own and to have the flexibility that I have."

In particular, Beni enjoys the ability to set her own hours. She elaborates, "My schedule is dictated by the kids. When my daughter was younger, and she stayed home, I either worked from home (versus at the client site) or I didn't work at all on those days. Now that my children are older and in school, I am free to work more. My workload has increased gradually, based on the number of days my daughter attends school. If I told a client that I could only work two days per week they would accept that. I can take off to be at a school function, meet my kids for lunch, or stay home with them when they're sick. One of us (me or my husband) is there for every single school event (plays, activities, etc.). I juggle my business around my children's activities."

Beni's flexible schedule allows her to take off large blocks of time to spend with her family. Last summer, she took off and went to Colorado for the entire summer.

Beni comments excitedly, "It was the greatest thing! I am not going to work summers anymore! I made a conscious decision not to work. It was so wonderful getting to spend time with my daughters without looking at my watch and worrying about meeting with a client. I even took my workstation with me but as it turned out, I only billed four hours all summer. Right now, I am working five days a week to wrap up a project. If I work longer now, I will be able to take off several months this summer to go to Washington State."

Beni's decision to work part time reminds us that not all women are cut out to be full-time stay-at-home moms. She explains, "I could not give up my work completely to stay home. I personally need the mental stimulation of my work. If I stayed home as a full-time mom, then it would be detrimental to my whole family. I see a lot of women who do stay home who are depressed, and they may not even know it. Full-time moms have a very different social structure. They talk about kid's clothes and what they eat, etc. vs. designing a database. I need to do business things to keep my mind active."

Beni offers some advice to other women who are thinking about going out on their own. "If you're thinking of being in business for yourself, especially if you want to be a mother, do it! If it works out, the gains are great. If you're afraid of taking risks, plan for it in advance. If you've built up savings, it is less of a risk. If you contemplate it forever, you will never do it."

"You must be disciplined. When I first started out, the discipline was more of an adjustment for me than the money or even the start-up costs. Some of my clients salivate over my situation, but they want that steady paycheck every month. It keeps them from going out on their own. Try it for one year, after that you can always go back and get a job. If you keep learning new skills, you can add them to your resume so you are more marketable. It is very important to keep your skills up to date – take numerous classes and attend all the conferences, seminars, and workshops that you can. Another thing I would say is that you must have the support of your family, in particular your spouse. I would like to take this opportunity to thank my husband for all his support and help in this venture."

For Beni Patel, her decision to go out on her own has paid off in big ways. She has the freedom and flexibility she needs in her life to work part time and spend time with her family. Beni sums it up best when she says "I'm not working for money, I am working for a lifestyle."

Many thanks to my friend and colleague Beni Patel, who can be reached at: beni@bigfoot.com

CHAPTER 16

(The Pros and Cons of) Working from Home

So how do you keep from going crazy if you work out of the house? Obviously, there are pros and cons to working from home. This short chapter provides viewpoints from both sides of the debate.

ADVANTAGES OF WORKING FROM HOME

It goes without saying that there are certain advantages to working from home. Number one, it is cost-effective. It is easy and inexpensive to set up a home office. There are no overhead costs. You can convert an entire bedroom, part of a bedroom, or even a closet into a partial office. Ann Kasunich, a marketing professional profiled in Chapter 10, fashioned an office by stringing up a curtain as a divider in one of her bedrooms.

The second benefit is that there is no commute. Your commute is as long as a walk across your living room. Not to mention that you save on gasoline and drive time that you can use to do something else.

A third benefit, one you may not have considered, is that a home office is a tax write-off. You are eligible to take a percentage (the square footage of your office divided by the total square footage of your house) of your mortgage interest, homeowners insurance, and utility bills as a deduction on your annual federal income taxes.

DON'T BLUR WORK AND HOME LIFE

It seems that Ann Kasunich's curtain served another purpose: to keep the lines between work and home life from becoming too blurred. When working from home, there are already too many distractions as it is, and it is tempting to do chores around the house, to put in a load of laundry or run the vacuum, for instance. The trick is to put yourself in a business frame of mind and separate home life from work.

Another purported benefit to working out of the house, is that you can keep your kids at home and watch them while you work. But is this really realistic? Many women have told me it doesn't work to have your kids at home while you work, that it is not conducive to maintaining a business or professional atmosphere, and it is difficult to get any work done.

With a newborn, you must have dedicated time for a baby. Initially, when babies sleep for 3 or 4 hours at a stretch, you can stay home with your child, and work while the baby is sleeping (if you're not too tired!). But as babies grow older and become more active, that becomes more difficult. Even having an in-house nanny has its share of problems, especially if the child is aware that "Mommy is home" and cries to see you while you are working.

If you do decide to work at home with your family present, set some definite boundaries. Because it is difficult to quickly transition mentally from consultant-mode to home-life mode, establish some ground rules. For instance, if your husband gets home from work and you are still working, a closed office door means that you are still "in work mode," even though he is not. Set aside some dedicated time each day when you can talk on the phone without distractions.

Beni Patel, an independent consultant profiled in the previous chapter, says, "Teach your children that work is important to you and that they need to respect your workspace. Set aside a place in your home that is your office and when you are in the office, the children know you are at work. I have taught my kids that when my office door is shut, that means that 'Mommy is at work,' and they know not to bother me."

The toughest adjustment to working from home is a mental one. It is difficult to go from the corporate workplace and a professional atmosphere to a home office. It is quite a contrast, so expect and plan for some transition time.

CABIN FEVER

Another reality of a home office is the lack of socialization, and the isolation that comes from not being around co-workers during the day. For many consultants, this balances out due to the time they spend on-site at a client's office. For many instructors, the amount of time spent at home is offset by the time spent at a client site teaching a class.

It also helps if you do most of your social interaction at night, rather than during the day. For instance, get out of the house and go out to dinner after work. Have several activities that you participate regularly in after work. Before I had my daughter, I played tennis with friends in a league, and I also sat on a city board that met several nights each month.

Keep in mind that everybody has her own limits. Leita Hart, a CPA profiled in Chapter 5, says, "I am well-suited for working out of the house. I like it. I was an only child. There's been times when it's been hard, but I can always meet someone for lunch. I like the quiet, solitary environment of my home office (versus the corporate office). Trust me, there's no isolation with a family around!"

Tina Brown, a consultant who works from home every other week (see Chapter 7), offers this insight into working from home: "I do office out of my house. I don't feel isolated because I get the social aspect of work every other week. I am not home every other week. I find it refreshing because I can get a lot done when I am in the office. I also have a separate office. I get up in the morning, exercise, get dressed, and go into my office to work. My office was built as an office (vs. a converted bedroom), and that makes all the difference."

Cynthia Long, a computer project manager profiled in Chapter 3, works out of her house, but finds it necessary to be around people. She says, "Because of the kind of work I do [IT], I am with people a lot. I talk on the phone and meet with people. I need people around because I enjoy the synergy that comes from working with other people." As a project manager, Cynthia often finds herself in the position of giving orders. Laughing, she says, "My husband tells me that I'm good at telling other people what to do!"

OTHER OPTIONS

If working from home is not for you, then another option is to look into leasing or subletting an office. Many times companies will have empty offices they will sublease. An executive suite is also a good option, because it allows you to lease an individual office, but then share common areas (kitchen, conference rooms) with other tenants. Executive suites are available through management companies at office buildings. Rates vary, depending on many factors, including location.

I rented an executive suite a few years ago, and found that this arrangement worked very well for me. Not only was I around other professional people during the day, but when I was at the office, I found I was actually more productive (because I knew I was there to work). Having an office away from the house shields you from distracting and unwanted phone calls from your home telephone, and provides a professional location for client meetings.

Ann Kasunich, who has been working out of her house since 2001, says, "Working out of the house worked really well for the first few years. But there are times when it drives me crazy being home all day. I have considered renting an executive suite, but at the same time, by working out of the house, I don't have that overhead."

She continues, "So when I find myself feeling aggravated by working out of my bedroom office, I work at determining the source of my frustration and adjust accordingly. Most of the time I need to adjust my organization system, office hours, and/or work load. The important part is to recognize that your company needs and your family needs are dynamic. If things aren't working, determine what is wrong and try something else. The one guarantee is that there will be lots of change, and you need to be flexible."

SELF-DISCIPLINE

One thing about working at home is that there isn't any boss looking over your shoulder, so it's up to you to sit down and get the work done. Unfortunately, there are many potential distractions around the house. It can be very tempting to do household chores, putter in the garden, or even watch TV during the day.

It takes self-discipline and maturity to resist these temptations. As suggested in Chapter 1, it helps to set a work schedule and regular office hours. Get up at the same time every day and get dressed for work. This helps to put you in a business frame of mind.

Ann Kasunich offers some parting wisdom regarding self-discipline, "Flexibility is a responsibility that needs to be managed. You need to be disciplined and focused on what needs to get done and then set the framework (lists, schedules, whatever works for the individual) to get it done."

In closing, there are pros and cons to working from home, just like there are pros and cons to self-employment. Ultimately you will never know how you will react to a situation until you actually try it. The women I have talked to who have done it are happy with their lifestyles and the choices they made. It is my sincere hope that if you decide to try this, that you will be too.

CHAPTER 17

Advice from Those Who've Been There

The title of this final chapter is self-explanatory. Many of us starting a business wish we had a mentor, an experienced person able to give us advice about the problems and challenges we're about to face. This chapter features lessons learned the hard way, not only by myself, but also by other women who learned from experience.

ESTABLISHING PRIORITIES IN BUSINESS

As stated previously, you must make your business a priority. As a business owner, there are several specific tasks that should take priority over all else.

TOP FIVE PRIORITIES FOR A BUSINESS OWNER

1. Finding clients and serving their needs.
2. Getting paid for your services.
3. Keeping accurate business records (see Chapter 2).
4. Paying your bills and making a profit.
5. Keeping up to date with software and technology in your field.

Once you go out on your own, it is up to you to bring in new business. If you don't have any sales or business development experience, this is a whole new world for you. One of your priorities should be finding the business and serving your clients' needs, which actually means doing the work.

Chapter 4, "Selling Yourself," offers advice on networking, finding new business, and other methods of selling yourself and your services. Another important aspect of being on your own is getting paid, paying your bills, and making a profit. Why be in business for yourself if you're not making any money?

Finally, as an independent, it will be completely up to you to keep yourself up to date with new software and technology. It is important to keep on learning new skills in order to maintain your marketability. (For more on this topic, see Chapter 14 – Being a Professional.)

FEAST OR FAMINE

Business is cyclical. That is the nature of the beast.

Depending upon the services you offer, your business may be affected by various budget cycles. Typically, a state agency's fiscal year (FY) ends on August 31 of any given year, and the federal government's FY ends on September 30. Usually, in the months leading up to the end of the fiscal year, state and federal governments are frantically searching for ways to spend money prior to the new budget year.

This is commonly known as "use it or lose it," because frequently, if the money is not spent, these agencies will not receive the same amount of money in their budget for the next FY. This is good news for trainers and for those who sell products, software or equipment. Because I live in Austin, the state capital of Texas and consequently where many state agencies are headquartered, I receive a lot of requests for classes every August.

Another reason business is cyclical is that it may be seasonal. A landscape business for example, may make most of its money during the spring and summer months, when demand is high, rather than during the cold winter months. Because my GPS classes are held outdoors, I teach most of these in the spring, early summer, or fall, before the weather gets too hot or too cold. For CPAs, usually the first quarter of the year before April 15 is their busiest time, during tax season.

Be prepared for dry spells. In the second quarter of 2002, the economy was very soft (six months after Sept. 11, 2001), and I didn't teach a single class. While I was ready for this contingency financially, I found I was unprepared mentally for the downtime. During those three months I did a lot of marketing. Thankfully, I did have some writing business (several articles and brochures) that came my way.

Another thing to keep in mind is that December is the slowest month for almost all businesses. People are thinking about things other than work, mainly the approaching holidays.

A wise man (my father) once told me, "You must make enough money when times are good in order to make it through the slow times." This is a different way of saying "Make hay while the sun shines." My father has had his own engineering business since 1973, and his business survived some tough economic recessions.

It is not uncommon for a trainer to teach several classes one month, and only one or even none the next. One trainer told me he made $9000 in one month, and I know another instructor who made $20,000 in a single month. The trick is to build up a cushion of savings during your productive months in order to make it through the slow periods. (At the end of the year, put the extra money into your SEP IRA – see Chapter 2.)

If you are an even-tempered person who can keep your nerve, then you will weather the times when your income is low (or sometimes nothing at all).

THE ART OF CONTRACT NEGOTIATION

Most of us don't have a lot of experience negotiating contracts. Some women are intimidated just thinking about it, while others are too eager to "be nice" and allow an opposing party to get whatever they want in order to avoid conflict.

When you go into business for yourself, contract negotiation is a fact of life. If you don't stand up for yourself, you will get a raw deal. What follows are some tips and helpful lessons I have learned from firsthand experience.

Generally speaking, a contract is a simple document that spells out the tasks and deliverables expected of both parties entering into the agreement. Typically a contract favors the party who is writing the contract or making the offer. Of course, you want it to be a "win-win" situation for both parties (otherwise why do the work?), but the reality is that a contract is written to favor the issuing party. The person on the receiving end of the contract must make more concessions.

Unfortunately, a former colleague of mine did not understand this basic principle. I had asked her to do some subcontract work for me, and I had a lawyer write a contract containing a very strict non-compete clause. I had already been burned once before by a subcontractor who went out from under me and started working for my client directly. I certainly didn't intend for that to happen again!

When I sent the contract over to her, she asked her own lawyer to look it over (fair enough). However, her lawyer completely rewrote the entire contract in her favor and sent it back to me. I told her that I was not open to making any substantial changes in the document, and that was the end of the agreement and our association. Instead of asking for incremental changes, she wanted to change everything at once, which left no room to negotiate. Ultimately, she lost out, because I kept the business (and the money!) for myself.

Lesson learned? Know when to compromise. Don't push the issue unless it is something you really can't live without.

At the same time, if a contract doesn't include a clause that you would like to add, request it. (Just don't rewrite the entire document). Say something like, "I would like to add a clause pertaining to . . . ." Just because something isn't in the initial write-up doesn't mean it can't be added.

On the other hand, just because something is in writing, doesn't mean it can't be changed. Business contracts are not as inflexible as they might seem. There is give and take on both sides – just be reasonable. Any agreement is considered "in progress" until both parties sign on the dotted line.

All contracts should contain a confidentiality clause. Because client lists, rates, and pay scales, along with everything else, are discussed between you and your subcontractor, you don't want that sensitive information to be shared with third parties.

Finally, make sure that all contracts contain the following statement, "It is understood that each party works as an independent contractor, and shall not be considered an employee of the other." This is self-explanatory, in order to maintain your status as a self-employed person.

NEGOTIATING SKILLS

Attending a contract negotiation to finalize a sale with a client can be very intimidating. After all, it's your livelihood on the line. It helps to be prepared.

Cynthia Long, a computer project manager featured in Chapter 3, offers some insight on meetings and negotiating tactics. She says, "One thing I have learned is never go into a meeting where the other person knows the agenda and you don't. It's easy to get ambushed that way."

Don't get your emotions involved when negotiating a contract (this is a good life lesson in general, even for something as mundane as buying a car). Separate yourself from your emotions, and use your intellect to think logically and rationally. This is difficult for most women to do. By keeping a "poker face" you won't reveal your stance on an issue too early, which puts you in a better bargaining position (because the other side won't know how much something does or doesn't mean to you).

If for some reason the meeting doesn't turn out in your favor, know your fallback position, as in what you can live with at a bare minimum if everything falls through. Another basic negotiating skill is that if you make a concession to appease a client, it is fair to ask for something in return. Sometimes, for instance, you may have to offer a lower rate just to get your foot in the door. After six months to a year, once you have proven yourself and your worth, renegotiate the contract at a higher rate.

TIMING IS EVERYTHING

Keep in mind that timing is everything. Your tone of voice, and *how* and *when* you say something can impact the outcome of a meeting. Do you think that Neil Armstrong said his famous line "One small step for man, one giant leap for mankind" off the top of his head? I have never asked him, but I am sure he thought that out way in advance, and waited for the perfect moment to *deliver* it.

Once, on a cruise, my husband wanted to purchase a bottle of expensive Scotch. The price was very high, and we talked to another passenger who said he had offered less, and the shop attendant had sold it to him for the lesser price.

Armed with this information, we strolled to the liquor shop, only to find it full of people making last-minute purchases. Because the shop was so crowded, my husband's offer fell on deaf ears. In hindsight, we should have waited until the shop was deserted, when we had a much better chance of getting what we wanted. With a shop full of paying customers, the shop-keeper had no incentive to lower his price.

SOMETIMES YOU HAVE TO BE AN @$$#*[Σ!

My husband told me this simple secret. In other words, know what you won't give up, and stand your ground. This comes easier for men than women.

By nature, most women are accommodating, wanting everybody to get along. This does not always work in a contract negotiation setting. If something is important to you, don't abandon it and give in. However uncomfortable it may be, sometimes you must hang tough. Negotiating a contract can be difficult the first time around, but overall the experience will contribute to your character and personal growth.

One last thing: Know when enough is enough. Sometimes a contract can have a "deal breaker" that makes it not worth pursuing. If the contract requires that you make substantial changes, such as incorporating your business or obtaining liability insurance or a bond, then it may not be worth it to pursue the business. Know your limits. If something makes you uncomfortable (or is illegal), don't do it. As a colleague of mine once told me, "When it comes to business, no deal is better than a bad deal."

SIX THINGS TO REMEMBER WHEN NEGOTIATING CONTRACTS

1. Don't get your emotions involved.
2. Know when to compromise.
3. If something you want is not in the contract, ask for it.
4. If you make a concession to appease a client, ask for something in return.
5. Know your fallback position if you can't get everything you want.
6. Stand your ground and walk away if you have to.

ADVICE FROM OTHER WOMEN

A friend of mine, who recently accepted a full-time position with a large corporate employer after two years on her own, offers some advice about what she would have done differently. Celia Thompkins was laid off from a high-tech manufacturing company in October 2001, during an economic downturn. A CPA with many years of experience, she used her severance pay in early 2002 to purchase a franchise business specializing in leadership development.

Celia recommends that, in the beginning, you "Count the costs, then prepare. Know your industry, and know what it takes to be successful in it. Go test your ideas on clients, and get all the facts first. This is more than just market research, it's understanding the industry you're getting into.

I didn't really do that. After two years on my own, I found I was spending time trying to understand the industry, instead of getting clients. Although I was well known in the accounting field, I had to build an entirely new network for the leadership development market. You need to have clients lined up before you go out and take the plunge. There is nothing wrong with taking risks, but they need to be educated risks."

Celia continues, "Another thing I should have done is to announce to everyone I knew what I was going to do. A lot of people have a lot of great ideas, but then they don't tell anybody. Make a commitment to tell others. In the preparation phase, looking back, I should have worked on my selling skills. Build your network before you start the business. When you go out on your own, you need to take an honest assessment of yourself, and commit to personal development. If you're not good at selling, take some classes to brush up on your skills. I didn't do that either. Your source of drive is internal, and you must set your own schedules and stick to it."

RISK MANAGEMENT

Is there really such a thing as risk management? Perhaps not, but there are some steps you can take to limit your liability and risk in business. For example, subcontracting to a prime contractor shields you and limits your risk.

Deciding to make the change to a more flexible lifestyle is a risk in itself, but think of it as a calculated risk. The rewards far outweigh anything else. Below is a checklist of advice for starting out from the case studies in this book and others who have been there and done it.

ADVICE FOR GOING OUT ON YOUR OWN –
FIVE COMMON THEMES FROM WOMEN WHO HAVE DONE IT

1. Save enough money to live on during the start-up phase.
2. Network and call everyone you know.
3. Take a risk. Don't be scared – consider it a new challenge. Educate yourself and do your market research first to make sure there is demand for what you do, but otherwise go for it!
4. Have the self-discipline required to dedicate yourself to your business.
5. Work hard.

IN CLOSING

I have thoroughly enjoyed writing this book. I deliberately wrote it so it can be used as a reference (and made it a handy size that can be kept in a purse or briefcase), and have included specific tangible steps that you can put into action. I carefully selected each of the women profiled because of their experience, professionalism and success. May you benefit from their collective wisdom and lessons learned.

It is my sincere hope that I have given you the motivation to go out on your own, or at least start thinking about it. Even though starting a business takes a lot of advance planning and hard work, it is worthwhile to gain the rewards of working part time and/or a more flexible lifestyle. As downhill skiers say, "No guts, no glory!"

Appendix

Additional Resources

(Note: Listing does not imply endorsement.)

NATIONAL HISTORICALLY UNDERUTILIZED BUSINESS (HUB) REGISTRATION AGENCIES

Many organizations that contract with HUBs require individual certification (through their respective city or state). Some, however, are reciprocal, meaning they will accept a national HUB certification as an alternative to the multiple state and local certifications. Please check with your local entity for more information.

NATIONAL MINORITY SUPPLIER DEVELOPMENT COUNCIL, INC.
1040 Avenue of the Americas, 2nd Floor
New York, NY 10018
(212) 944-2430

NATIONAL WOMEN BUSINESS OWNERS CORPORATION (NWBOC)
1100 Wayne Ave., Suite 830
Silver Spring, MD 20910

SMALL BUSINESS ADMINISTRATION 8A BUSINESS
DEVELOPMENT CERTIFICATION PROGRAM
Contact Regional SBA Office

U.S. SMALL BUSINESS ADMINISTRATION HUBZONE PROGRAM
409 3rd Street S.W., 8th Floor
Washington, DC 20416
(202) 205-8885
hubzone@sba.gov

U.S. DEPARTMENT OF TRANSPORTATION
MINORITY OWNED BUSINESS CERTIFICATION PROGRAM
400 7th Street, S.W.
Washington, DC 20590
(202) 366-4000

WOMEN'S BUSINESS ENTERPRISE NATIONAL COUNCIL
1120 Connecticut Avenue, NW, Suite 1000
Washington, DC 20036
(202) 872-5515

HISTORICALLY UNDERUTILIZED BUSINESS (HUB), DISADVANTAGED BUSINESS ENTERPRISE (DBE), AND WOMAN OWNED (WO) REGISTRATION AGENCIES BY STATE

Note: Listing by state is not comprehensive. In addition to state HUB certification, many municipal governments and regional authorities (e.g., transportation, airport, or other) will grant HUB status. Please research the city where
you live, and/or any regional authorities in your area. If your state is not listed
here, you may have to explore national certifications.

ARIZONA
CITY OF PHOENIX, MINORITY, WOMAN, DISADVANTAGED,
AND SMALL BUSINESS ENTERPRISE CERTIFICATION
Phoenix City Hall
200 W. Washington St.
Phoenix, AZ 85003
www.azcommerce.com

ARKANSAS STATE HIGHWAY AND TRANSPORTATION DEPARTMENT
P.O. Box 2261
Little Rock, AR 72203
(501) 569-2000
www.ahtd.state.ar.us

CALIFORNIA DEPARTMENT OF GENERAL SERVICES (DGS)
Office of Small Business and DVBE (Disabled Veteran
Business Enterprise) Certification
P.O. Box 989052
West Sacramento, CA 95798-9052
www.dgs.ca.gov

CALIFORNIA DEPARTMENT OF TRANSPORTATION (CALTRANS)
CALIFORNIA UNIFIED CERTIFICATION PROGRAM (CUCP)
Civil Rights MS 79
1823 14th Street
Sacramento, CA 95814
(916) 324-1700 or
(866) 810-6346 Toll Free
www.dot.ca.gov

COLORADO DEPARTMENT OF TRANSPORTATION
UNIFIED CERTIFICATION PROGRAM (UCP)
Office of Certification
4201 E. Arkansas, EMP B600
Denver, CO 80222
(303) 512-4140

CONNECTICUT DEPARTMENT OF TRANSPORTATION
Bureau of Finance & Administration
2800 Berlin Turnpike
Newington, CT 06131-7546
(860) 594-2171
www.ct.gov/dot

DISTRICT OF COLUMBIA LOCAL BUSINESS OPPORTUNITY COMMISSION
Local, Small and Disadvantaged Business Enterprise Program
441 4th Street, NW, Suite 970N
Washington, DC 20001
(202) 727-3900

FLORIDA DEPARTMENT OF TRANSPORTATION
DISADVANTAGED BUSINESS ENTERPRISE PROGRAM
Equal Opportunity Office
605 Suwannee Street, MS 65
Tallahassee, FL 32399
(850) 414-4747

GEORGIA DEPARTMENT OF TRANSPORTATION
DISADVANTAGED BUSINESS ENTERPRISES
No. 2 Capitol Square, S.W.
Atlanta, GA 30334
(404) 656-5267

HAWAII DEPARTMENT OF TRANSPORTATION DBE PROGRAM
Aliiaimoku Building
869 Punchbowl Street
Honolulu, HI 96813
www.state.hi.us/dot/administration/dbe

HOUSTON MINORITY BUSINESS COUNCIL
6671 Southwest Freeway, Suite 110
Houston, TX 77074
www.hmbc.org

IDAHO TRANSPORTATION DEPARTMENT DBE PROGRAM
Administered through the U.S. Department of Transportation
(see National HUB Certifications)

ILLINOIS DEPARTMENT OF TRANSPORTATION DBE PROGRAM
Harry R. Hanley Building
2300 South Dirksen Parkway, Room 319
Springfield, IL 62764
(217) 785-5947
www.dot.state.il.us

INDIANA DEPARTMENT OF ADMINISTRATION MBE/WBE/DBE CERTIFICATION
Deputy Commissioner for Minority and Women's Business Enterprises
402 W. Washington Street W474
Indianapolis, IN 46204
(317) 232-3061
www.state.in.us/idoa/minority/index.html

IOWA DEPARTMENT OF TRANSPORTATION
DOT Office of Contracts, EEO Section
800 Lincoln Way
Ames, IA 50010
(515) 239-1422
www.dot.state.ia.us

KANSAS STATEWIDE CERTIFICATION PROGRAM
via Kansas Department of Commerce and Kansas Department of Transportation
Office of Minority & Women Business
1000 S.W. Jackson St., Suite 100
Topeka, KS 66612-1354
(785) 296-5298
www.ksdot.org

KENTUCKY ECONOMIC DEVELOPMENT CABINET
Small and Minority Business Division
67 Wilkinson Blvd.
(502) 564-2064
(877) 355-3822 Toll Free
Frankfort, KY 40601
www.thinkkentucky.com/SMBD

LOUISIANA MINORITY BUSINESS COUNCIL
(504) 523-7110
www.lambc.org

LOUISIANA WOMEN'S BUSINESS COUNCIL WOMEN OWNED CERTIFICATION
(504) 680-1886
www.wbcgulfcoast.org

LOUISIANA DEPARTMENT OF TRANSPORTATION &
DEVELOPMENT (DOTD) DBE PROGRAM
(225) 379-1444 or
(225) 379-1382
www.dotd.louisiana.gov

MAINE DEPARTMENT OF TRANSPORTATION DBE PROGRAM
Office of Human Resources
#16 State House Station
Augusta, ME 04333-0016
(207) 624-3066
www.maine.gov/mdot-stage

MARYLAND DEPARTMENT OF TRANSPORTATION MBE/DBE PROGRAM
Minority Business Enterprise Office
7201 Corporate Center Drive
P.O. Box 548
Hanover, MD 21076
(410) 865-1269
(800) 544-6056 Toll Free
mbe@mdot.state.md.us
www.mdot.state.md.us

MASSACHUSETTS STATE OFFICE OF MINORITY AND
WOMEN BUSINESS ASSISTANCE (SOMWBA)
10 Park Plaza, Suite 3740
Boston, MA 02116
(617) 973-8692
wsomwba@state.ma.us

MICHIGAN DEPARTMENT OF TRANSPORTATION
Michigan Unified Certification Program (MUCP)
425 W. Ottawa
P.O. Box 30050
Lansing, MI 48909
(517) 335-0945 or
(866) 323-1264 Toll Free
mdot-dbe@michigan.gov
www.michigan.gov/mdot

MINNESOTA DEPARTMENT OF ADMINISTRATION MATERIALS MANAGEMENT
DIVISION TARGETED GROUP/ECONOMICALLY DISADVANTAGED (TG/ED)
SMALL BUSINESS PROGRAM
(651) 296-2600
mmdhelp.line@state.mn.us
www.mmd.admin.state.mn.us

MISSISSIPPI DEPARTMENT OF TRANSPORTATION DBE PROGRAM
Office of Civil Rights
ATTN: Carr Murphy
P.O. Box 1850
Jackson, MS 39215-1850
(601) 359-7466
cmurphy@mdot.state.ms.us
www.mdot.state.ms.us

MISSOURI OFFICE OF ADMINISTRATION OFFICE OF EQUAL OPPORTUNITY
P.O. Box 809
Jefferson City, MO 65102
(573) 751-8130 or
(877) 259-2963 Toll Free
www.oa.state.mo.us/oeo

MONTANA DEPARTMENT OF TRANSPORTATION DBE PROGRAM
P.O. Box 201001
2701 Prospect Ave.
Helena, MT 59620-1001
Leslie R. Wootan, DBE Program Manager
(406) 444-6337
lwootan@state.mt.us
or
Alice Flesch, DBE Program Specialist
(406) 444-9229
aflesch@state.mt.us
www.mdt.state.mt.us

NEBRASKA DEPARTMENT OF ROADS (NDOR)
DBE Office
P.O. Box 94759
Lincoln, NE 68509-4759
www.dor.state.ne.us

NEBRASKA DEPARTMENT OF ECONOMIC DEVELOPMENT
http://assist.neded.org/mincert.html

NEW HAMPSHIRE DEPARTMENT OF TRANSPORTATION DBE PROGRAM
Jay Ankenbrock, DBE Coordinator
P.O. Box 483
1 Hazen Drive
Concord, NH 03302-0483
(603) 271-6612
www.nh.gov/dot

NEW MEXICO DEPARTMENT OF TRANSPORTATION
OFFICE OF EQUAL OPPORTUNITY
1596 Pacheo Aspen Plaza
Santa Fe, NM 87501
(505) 827-1774
(800) 544-0936 Toll Free
www.nmshtd.state.nm.us

NEW YORK STATE DEPARTMENT OF TRANSPORTATION
Office of Equal Opportunity Development & Compliance
(518) 457-1129
www.dot.state.ny.us

NEW YORK
EMPIRE STATE DEVELOPMENT CORPORATION
(800) 782-8369 Toll Free
www.nylovesbiz.com

NORTH CAROLINA DEPARTMENT OF TRANSPORTATION
Civil Rights & Business Development Section
P.O. Box 25201
Raleigh, NC 27611-5201
(919) 733-2300
(800) 522-0453 Toll Free
www.ndot.org

NORTH DAKOTA DEPARTMENT OF TRANSPORTATION DBE PROGRAM
608 East Boulevard Avenue
Bismarck, ND 58505-0700
Deborah J. Igoe, DBE Liaison Officer
(701) 328-2576
digoe@state.nd.us
or
Marlene Larson, Civil Rights Officer
(701) 328-3116
mlarson@state.nd.us
www.state.nd.us/dot/

OHIO DEPARTMENT OF ADMINISTRATIVE SERVICES
320 Arthur E. Adams Drive
Columbus, OH 43221-3595
(614) 466-8380
www.das.ohio.gov

OKLAHOMA DEPARTMENT OF TRANSPORTATION
Regulatory Services
200 N.E. 21st Street, Room 1-C-5
Oklahoma City, OK 73105
(405) 521-6046
(800) 788-4539 Toll Free
www.okladot.state.ok.us

OREGON OFFICE OF MINORITY, WOMEN, AND EMERGING SMALL BUSINESS
P.O. Box 14480
Salem, OR 97309-0405
(503) 947-7922
www.cbs.state.or.us/omwesb

PENNSYLVANIA DEPARTMENT OF GENERAL SERVICES
Room 502 North Office Building
Harrisburg, PA 17125
(717) 787-6708
www.dgs.state.pa.us

RHODE ISLAND MINORITY BUSINESS ENTERPRISE
Minority Business Enterprise Compliance Office
One Capitol Hill
2nd Floor
Providence, RI 02908
(401) 222-6670
www.rimbe.org

SOUTH CAROLINA DEPARTMENT OF TRANSPORTATION DBE PROGRAM
955 Park Street
P.O. Box 191
Columbia, SC 29202-0191
(803) 737-2314
www.dot.state.sc.us

SOUTH CENTRAL TEXAS REGIONAL CERTIFICATION AGENCY
301 S. Frio Suite 106
San Antionio, TX 78207
(210) 227-4722

SOUTH DAKOTA DEPARTMENT OF TRANSPORTATION
MBE COMPLIANCE PROGRAM
Denise Voorhes, DBE Compliance Officer
(605) 773-4906
Denise.Voorhes@state.sd.us
www.sddot.com

TENNESSEE DEPARTMENT OF TRANSPORTATION
Civil Rights Division
Small Business Development
(615) 741-3681
www.tdot.state.tn.us/civil-rights/Smallbusiness.htm

TEXAS DEPARTMENT OF TRANSPORTATION DBE CERTIFICATION PROGRAM
125 E. 11th Street
Austin, TX 78701-2483
(512) 703-5830
www.dot.state.tx.us

TEXAS BUILDING AND PROCUREMENT COMMISSION (FORMERLY GENERAL
SERVICES COMMISSION) MBE/WBE/HUB CERTIFICATION
P.O. Box 13047
Austin, TX 78701-3047
(512) 463-5872

UTAH DEPARTMENT OF TRANSPORTATION MBE PROGRAM
4501 South 2700 West
Mail Stop 141200
Salt Lake City, UT 84114-1200
(801) 965-4000
www.dot.state.ut.us

VERMONT AGENCY OF TRANSPORTATION (VTRANS)
Office of Civil Rights & Labor Compliance
National Life Bldg., Drawer 33
Montpelier , VT 05633-5001
(802) 828-2715
www.aot.state.vt.us/CivilRights/Dbe.htm

VIRGINIA DEPARTMENT OF MINORITY BUSINESS ENTERPRISE
200-202 North 9th Street, 11th Floor
Richmond, VA 23219
(800) 223-0671 (Toll Free in Virginia Only)
(804) 786-6585
www.dmbe.state.va.us

WASHINGTON STATE OFFICE OF MINORITY & WOMEN'S BUSINESS ENTERPRISE
Olympia, WA
(360) 753-9693
www.omwbe.wa.gov

WISCONSIN DEPARTMENT OF ADMINISTRATION
MINORITY BUSINESS PURCHASING PROGRAM
101 East Wilson Street
Room 621
P.O. Box 7867
Madison, WI 53707-7867
(608) 267-7806
www.doa.state.wi.us

WISCONSIN DEPARTMENT OF TRANSPORTATION DBE PROGRAM
4802 Sheboygan Ave.
Madison, WI 53705
(608) 266-7804
www.dot.state.wi.us

WYOMING DEPARTMENT OF TRANSPORTATION DBE PROGRAM
5300 Bishop Blvd.
Cheyenne, WY 82009-3340
(307) 777-4375
http://wydotweb.state.wy.us

NETWORKING ORGANIZATIONS

WOMEN IN TECHNOLOGY INTERNATIONAL (WITI)
WITI is an organization dedicated to helping women advance by providing access to – and support from – other professional women working in all sectors of technology.
Check www.witi.com for information about local chapter meetings.

EWOMENNETWORK, INC.
With events nationwide, eWomenNetwork, Inc. is the fastest growing membership-based professional women's networking organization in North America.
14900 Landmark Boulevard, Suite 540
Dallas, TX 75254
Check http://ewomennetwork.com for a listing of local events in your area.

HOME BASED WORKING MOMS
An online professional association providing support, networking, information, publicity opportunities, work opportunities, a monthly (print) newsletter, a weekly e-newsletter, member's listserv, panel of experts, and online membership directory.
www.hbwm.com

MOTHERS' HOME BUSINESS NETWORK
The (first and) largest national organization providing ideas, inspiration and support for mothers who choose to work at home.
www.homeworkingmom.com

AMERICAN SOCIETY OF TRAINING & DEVELOPMENT (ASTD)
ASTD is a leading association of professional trainers, instructors, and workplace learning and performance professionals.
1640 King Street, Box 1443
Alexandria, VA 22313-2043
(703) 683-8100
Check http://www.astd.org/astd for regional events and local chapter information.

BUSINESS NETWORK INTERNATIONAL (BNI)
World's largest referral organization.
545 College Commerce Way
Upland, CA 91786
(800) 825-8286 (Toll Free Outside Southern California)
(909) 608-7575 (Inside Southern California)
Check www.bni.com to find a local chapter in your area.

LEAD'S CLUBS OF THE MID-ATLANTIC
P.O. Box 607
Riva, MD 21140
(410) 956-5037
www.leadsclub.org

TOASTMASTERS INTERNATIONAL
Toastmasters is the premier organization for budding public speakers. Members learn by speaking to groups and working with others in a supportive environment.
Check www.toastmasters.org for more information.

NATIONAL SPEAKER'S ASSOCIATION (NSA)
NSA is the leading organization for professional speakers.
Check www.nsaspeaker.org for information regarding local chapter meetings.

GIRLSTART
For mothers who want to encourage their daughters to pursue a high-tech career from an early age, Girlstart is a non-profit organization created to empower girls to excel in math, science, and technology. Founded in 1997 in Austin, Texas, Girlstart engages, educates, and motivates girls to achieve the knowledge and confidence to participate in advanced math and science classes and future careers. Offering workshops, technology camps, and other fun, creative, and innovative ways to introduce girls to technology. *See www.girlstart.org for more information.*

BID OPPORTUNITIES AND ONLINE MARKETPLACE LISTINGS

HUBZONE
The HUBZone Empowerment Contracting program provides federal contracting opportunities for qualified small businesses. Provides a listing of all federal contracts currently available to HUBS.
Go to www.sba.gov/hubzone for more information.

DEPARTMENT OF ENERGY INTERACTIVE PROCUREMENT SYSTEM
http://doe-iips.pr.doe.gov

FEDERAL MARKETPLACE
Subscription service for federal Web-based government bid information.
www.fedmarket.com

FEDERAL BUSINESS OPPORTUNITIES
FedBizOpps is the single government point-of-entry (GPE) for federal government procurement opportunities over $25,000.
www.eps.gov

INPUT
Provides market forecasts and other tools to help technology vendors successfully compete in the federal marketplace and bid on government contracts.
www.input.com

STATE OF INDIANA PROCUREMENT PAGE
www.state.in.us/cgi-bin/idoa/cgi-bin/bidad.pl

INDIANA DEPARTMENT OF ADMINISTRATION
PUBLIC WORKS DIVISION CURRENT BID PROJECTS
www.state.in.us/serv/dapw_bviewer

STATE OF KENTUCKY E-PROCUREMENT PAGE
https://eProcurement.ky.gov

NEW MEXICO PROCUREMENT ASSISTANCE PROGRAM
P.O. Drawer 26110
Santa Fe, NM 87502-0110
(505) 827-0425
www.state.nm.us/spd/pap/index.html

TEXAS MARKETPLACE
Lists state government contracts and procurement opportunities for vendors.
www.marketplace.state.tx.us

WASHINGTON STATE
www.omwbe.wa.gov
click on "Bid Lists and Contracting Opportunities"

FRANCHISES AND OTHER BUSINESS OPPORTUNITIES

FRANCHISE DIRECT
Provides information and a directory of franchise opportunities.
www.franchisedirect.com

FRANCHISING.COM
website includes detailed information about various franchising and
business opportunities, informative franchising articles, and other franchise
related resources.
www.franchising.com

COMPUTER MOMS
Mentors On the Move (MOMs) is a home-based business franchise
specializing in providing one-on-one computer training at the client's
home or place of business.
www.computermoms.com

LEADERSHIP MANAGEMENT, INC.
Founded in 1965, LMI helps companies develop leadership skills in their employees. The company provides a line of programs and courses designed to help people achieve their professional and personal goals.
4567 Lake Shore Dr.
Waco, TX 76710
(800) 568-1241 Toll Free
www.lmi-bus.com

DALE CARNEGIE
Founded in 1912, the Dale Carnegie Institute provides self-improvement and leadership training. Franchises available.
www.dalecarnegie.com

DiSC TRAINING AND MATERIALS
DiSC training focuses on human behavior in order to help people understand "why they do what they do." The dimensions of Dominance, influencing, Steadiness, and Conscientiousness (DiSC) make up the model and interact with other factors to describe human behavior. Upon successful completion of DiSC's Train-the-Trainer course, you may use DiSC materials to teach the model.
www.resourcesunlimited.com/discprofilecert.asp

COACHVILLE
The largest professional network and trainer of coaches worldwide, CoachVille is a resource that provides training to all levels of coaches, from beginning to advanced.
www.cvcommunity.com

COACH TRAINING ALLIANCE
Provides training and certification to all levels of coaches.
www.coachtrainingalliance.com

CAREERS FROM HOME
Online career website specializing in connecting companies with individuals seeking flexible and alternative working conditions from a typical 40 hour work week.
www.careersfromhome.com

SOFTWARE CERTIFICATIONS
Provides IT certifications in three areas: Certified Software Project Manager (CSPM), Certified Software Quality Analyst (CSQA), and Certified Software Tester (CSTE).
www.softwarecertifications.com

Index

Book Order Forms

Book Order Form

YES! I would like to order _____ **copies of**
Full-Time Woman, Part-Time Career **at a cost
of $19.95 each plus $5 shipping and handling
for the first book and $2.50 for each book
thereafter.** (Texas residents please add 8.25 %
sales tax – $1.65)

My check or money order is enclosed.

Please charge my credit card:

❏ MasterCard   ❏ American Express
❏ VISA   ❏ Discover

Card # _____ Exp. Date _____

Signature _____

Total Amount to be Charged $ _____

Name _____

Address _____

City _____ State _____

Zip Code _____ Phone _____

E-mail _____

Please make your check payable to BookMasters, Inc., and mail along
with this form to:

BookMasters, Inc.
P.O. Box 388
Ashland, OH 44805

or

Order by phone at 1-800-247-6553
FAX this order form to 419-281-6883
By E-mail: order@bookmasters.com
www.atlasbooks.com

Book Order Form

YES! I would like to order _____ copies of *Full-Time Woman, Part-Time Career* at a cost of $19.95 each plus $5 shipping and handling for the first book and $2.50 for each book thereafter. (Texas residents please add 8.25 % sales tax – $1.65)

My check or money order is enclosed.

Please charge my credit card:

❑ MasterCard   ❑ American Express
❑ VISA   ❑ Discover

Card # _____ Exp. Date _____

Signature _____

Total Amount to be Charged $ _____

Name _____

Address _____

City _____ State _____

Zip Code _____ Phone _____

E-mail _____

Please make your check payable to BookMasters, Inc., and mail along with this form to:

BookMasters, Inc.
P.O. Box 388
Ashland, OH 44805

or

Order by phone at 1-800-247-6553
FAX this order form to 419-281-6883
By E-mail: order@bookmasters.com
www.atlasbooks.com

Book Order Form

YES! I would like to order _____ **copies of** *Full-Time Woman, Part-Time Career* **at a cost of $19.95 each plus $5 shipping and handling for the first book and $2.50 for each book thereafter.** (Texas residents please add 8.25 % sales tax – $1.65)

My check or money order is enclosed.

Please charge my credit card:

❏ MasterCard   ❏ American Express
❏ VISA   ❏ Discover

Card # _____ Exp. Date _____

Signature _____

Total Amount to be Charged $ _____

Name _____

Address _____

City _____ State _____

Zip Code _____ Phone _____

E-mail _____

Please make your check payable to BookMasters, Inc., and mail along with this form to:

BookMasters, Inc.
P.O. Box 388
Ashland, OH 44805

or

Order by phone at 1-800-247-6553
FAX this order form to 419-281-6883
By E-mail: order@bookmasters.com
www.atlasbooks.com

Book Order Form

YES! I would like to order _____ **copies of**
Full-Time Woman, Part-Time Career **at a cost**
of $19.95 each plus $5 shipping and handling
for the first book and $2.50 for each book
thereafter. (Texas residents please add 8.25 %
sales tax – $1.65)

My check or money order is enclosed.

Please charge my credit card:

❑ MasterCard ❑ American Express
❑ VISA ❑ Discover

Card # _____ Exp. Date _____

Signature _____

Total Amount to be Charged $ _____

Name _____

Address _____

City _____ State _____

Zip Code _____ Phone _____

E-mail _____

Please make your check payable to BookMasters, Inc., and mail along
with this form to:

BookMasters, Inc.
P.O. Box 388
Ashland, OH 44805

_or_

Order by phone at 1-800-247-6553
FAX this order form to 419-281-6883
By E-mail: order@bookmasters.com
www.atlasbooks.com

Book Order Form

YES! I would like to order _____ copies of *Full-Time Woman, Part-Time Career* at a cost of $19.95 each plus $5 shipping and handling for the first book and $2.50 for each book thereafter. (Texas residents please add 8.25 % sales tax – $1.65)

My check or money order is enclosed.

Please charge my credit card:

❏ MasterCard   ❏ American Express
❏ VISA   ❏ Discover

Card # _____ Exp. Date _____

Signature _____

Total Amount to be Charged $ _____

Name _____

Address _____

City _____ State _____

Zip Code _____ Phone _____

E-mail _____

Please make your check payable to BookMasters, Inc., and mail along with this form to:

BookMasters, Inc.
P.O. Box 388
Ashland, OH 44805

or

Order by phone at 1-800-247-6553
FAX this order form to 419-281-6883
By E-mail: order@bookmasters.com
www.atlasbooks.com

Book Order Form

YES! I would like to order _____ copies of _Full-Time Woman, Part-Time Career_ at a cost of $19.95 each plus $5 shipping and handling for the first book and $2.50 for each book thereafter. (Texas residents please add 8.25 % sales tax – $1.65)

My check or money order is enclosed.

Please charge my credit card:

❏ MasterCard   ❏ American Express
❏ VISA   ❏ Discover

Card # _____ Exp. Date _____

Signature _____

Total Amount to be Charged $ _____

Name _____

Address _____

City _____ State _____

Zip Code _____ Phone _____

E-mail _____

Please make your check payable to BookMasters, Inc., and mail along with this form to:

BookMasters, Inc.
P.O. Box 388
Ashland, OH 44805

or

Order by phone at 1-800-247-6553
FAX this order form to 419-281-6883
By E-mail: order@bookmasters.com
www.atlasbooks.com

ABOUT THE AUTHOR

Karen Steede Terry has been self-employed as an independent software instructor and consultant since 1996. Karen holds teaching certifications from four different GIS (Geographic Information Systems) and GPS (Global Positioning Systems) manufacturers. Previously, she was employed by ESRI®, Inc., and Trimble® Navigation, LTD., the market leading GIS and GPS companies, respectively.

She is a Trimble Certified Trainer, as well as an ESRI Authorized Instructor, and was the first woman to obtain both certifications. She also holds certifications from Leica Geosystems, Inc., and MapInfo® Corporation, and is the only person certified by all four manufacturers simultaneously.

GIS is a decision support tool that allows scientists or technicians to overlay map layers for querying data, analysis, mapping trends, and modeling scenarios. GIS and GPS are used worldwide in many different industries, a fact which is reflected in Karen's client base:

- SBC
- Pacific Bell
- The State of Texas
- Occidental Petroleum
- United Meridian Corporation

- XTO Energy
- 3D International
- Koch Industries Inc.
- Carter-Burgess, Inc.
- Numerous city and county governments

Karen is a graduate of Texas A&M University. A technical writer, she is published regularly in national trade magazines. Her first book, *Integrating GIS and the Global Positioning System,* was published in 2000 by the ESRI Press.

A member of the National Speakers Association (NSA), Karen is a regular speaker at GIS conferences. Here is some feedback from Karen's clients, students, and others who have heard her speak:

"One of the best speakers we've ever had!"
– Ross Epstein, Past President, Capital City A&M (Alumni) Club

"Karen is that rare combination of Subject Matter Expert (SME) who has good presentation skills."
– Harvey Browning, Recruiter, Texas Department of State Health Services

"Instructor is excellent, knowledgeable, and personable."
– John Gleason, City of Austin, Texas

"Karen was excellent – she did an outstanding job in explaining things, and was very patient."

– Ted Pearson, SBC

"Karen was very relaxed and confident in her delivery. She knew her material very well, and was very good in teaching that material."

– Tonya Chipley, SBC

"I was blown away by the quality of Karen's evaluations!"

– Ken Smith, Manager, Authorized Training Program, Texas Region

"One of the most popular speakers and workshops at our annual conference."

– Charles Fried, Chair, Petroleum User Group (PUG) Steering Committee

Karen Steede Terry was rated one of the Top 5 ESRI Instructors for First Quarter 2005 and Third Quarter 2004.

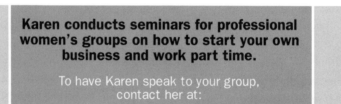

Karen conducts seminars for professional women's groups on how to start your own business and work part time.

To have Karen speak to your group, contact her at:

www.fulltimewoman.com
512-656-5032
info@fulltimewoman.com

Special Offer Coupon

Karen has recently begun to coach other women how to go out on their own. This coupon gives readers **one hour of coaching or consulting** with Karen at a **special introductory rate**.